Tactical Advantages from Gameboard to Life

CHECKMATE
MOVES FOR
BUSINESS
STARTUPS

WENDY OLIVERAS

CHECKMATE MOVES FOR BUSINESS STARTUPS

©2021, Wendy Oliveras

ISBN: 978-1-09835-411-4
ISBN eBook: 978-1-09835-412-1

Dedication

I dedicate this book to my beloved Daddy. It's been sixteen years since you departed from this earth and not one day goes by that I wish we could play a game of chess again. I will never forget those invaluable chess and life lessons you taught me throughout my life. I love you very much. Rest in eternal peace, Daddy!

Special Thanks

I give special thanks to the following individuals for providing me with their endless support of my Master SHESS Ideology and Pawn to SHESS Queen Theory. For this I am forever grateful!

Lorraine Santoli – You are an inspiration to me. Thank you for providing the Foreword, expert contribution to "Key Notes on Marketing and Branding," and editorial contributions.

Jorge Meneses, Esq. – I greatly appreciate your loyal friendship and professional legal counsel throughout these years.

Willa Edgerton-Chisler – Thank you, "amiga," for being such a great business coach and always believing in me. Your friendship and guidance in my life and career have been invaluable.

Arthur "Art" Jones – Thank you for your editorial contributions and helping me find my story to enhance my vision for SHESS! You are a true asset to my team.

Many thanks also go out to my colleagues, clients, affiliated partners, and educational institutions which have supported SHESS Global Alliance, LLC and my relentless passion to teach my Master SHESS Ideology and empowerment courses for women in business throughout these years. You know who you are!

Super Huge Thanks

Thank you to my beautiful mother Angeles, my rock Gladys, sisters Lillian and Freida, family, and friends for your endless patience, love, and support of my creative and professional endeavors. I love you all something awful!

Contributing Editors

Lorraine Santoli, Author of "Inside the Disney Marketing Machine"

Arthur "Art" Jones, Chief Story Architect, The Art of Standing Out, LLC

CONTENTS

FOREWORD 1

PREFACE 3

INTRODUCTION 9

PART 1
ANALOGIES INHERENT IN CHESS, LIFE, AND BUSINESS 17

PART 2
WOMEN IN BUSINESS AND THE MASTER SHESS IDEOLOGY 38

PART 3:
IDENTIFYING AND OBSERVING OPPONENTS IN LIFE AND BUSINESS 46

PART 4
ENDGAME VISIONARY STRATEGIES TO SET AND ACCOMPLISH GOALS 56

PART 5
SMART TACTICS TO HELP YOU SOLVE PROBLEMS 61

PART 6
STARTUP CHECKLIST FOR THE SHESS QUEEN IN BUSINESS 69

PART 7
TOP 10 MISTAKES YOU MUST AVOID IN BUSINESS 94

PART 8

BEST MOVES FOR YOUR FUTURE SUCCESS 102

PART 9

LEARN TO PLAY CHESS AND HAVE FUN! 105

About the Author 121

Great Resources 123

FOREWORD

Who would ever think that a woman's skill in the game of chess, considered a male-dominated sport, could catapult her to big-time business and life success? Wendy Oliveras, that's who. And as the author of this book, she will teach all the ladies (and men too!) how to do it as well.

I've known Wendy for over three decades through family connections, and I have always admired her tenacity, drive, and never-give-up attitude. She is a smart businesswoman that has many years of professional experience in the legal, intellectual property, small business consulting, Human Resources Management, educational, and leadership training fields. She holds a Master's Degree with honors in Human Resources Management, a post-graduate Certification in Career Planning and Development from The New School in New York City, and a Certification in Mental Health First Aid Training. She has also been playing the game of chess since she was a teenager.

Through her love and skillfulness of the game, which continues to grow to this day, she realized that the strategies, tactics, and problem-solving skills inherent in matching wits with an opponent, had more far-reaching benefits than just playing a game. It crossed over to a bigger gameboard—the business and life landscape—with particular focus on how it could empower women. In fact, after owning her own legal consulting firm, Oliveras & Company, Inc., for many years, it inspired her to start a new business called SHESS Global Alliance, LLC. The "SHESS" keyword, a combination of the words "she" and "chess," grew out of the concept of women learning chess to achieve greater success in business and in life.

Today, SHESS Global Alliance provides professional business advisory and training services for companies in the corporate, education, non-profit, and government sectors. Wendy is also an exceptional lead instructor and enjoys teaching life skills and chess to the inmate and community population at a corrections and rehabilitation center in New Jersey. To Wendy, there is no barrier in teaching how playing chess can be a strong motivator for growth despite personal challenges.

Wendy's passion for spreading the word about SHESS also turned her into a book author, with her first release, in 2012, entitled, "Let's Play SHESS - Succeed in your game of life and business by playing chess: from Pawn to Queen." Now, with the release of this new book, she details the "Pawn to SHESS Queen" process in a step-by-step narrative that offers readers further insight into the chess/business/life success model.

Included within the pages to follow: Analogies Inherent in Chess, Life, and Business; Women in Business and the SHESS Ideology; Identifying Opponents in Life and Business; Startup Checklist for the SHESS Queen; and so much more. It is a road map to achievement, accomplishment, and victory.

I, too, am a businesswoman, having had a twenty-two-year career as a PR and Marketing executive with The Walt Disney Company, as well as having written four published books, most recently, "Inside the Disney Marketing Machine." I understand the business landscape and recognize the powerful parallels of the game of chess to business and to life, as Wendy has illuminated in this text. I enjoyed the book immensely and even with my own extensive business experience, have gained valuable new insights from this book. I know you will too.

Lorraine Santoli,
November, 2020

PREFACE

WOW! It has been eight years since I published my first empowerment book, "Let's play SHESS," introducing the idea that chess, life, and business are interconnected, and playing chess for fun can help women succeed in life and business. So much has positively changed since then.

At that time, I was inspired to write the book due to personal and professional struggles I faced when the economic downturn hit in mid-2008. Just like a million others, I had to eventually close my legal staffing search firm business. There was a legal market hiring freeze across the nation. My clientele basically stopped hiring across the board.

I found myself in a precarious situation. I reassessed my financial needs and set new goals to help me survive and stay ahead of my game. Believe me when I tell you this was a very difficult time in my life. It wasn't easy, but I believed in myself and had the love and support of my amazing family, colleagues, and friends. I made a true commitment to myself not to allow this unexpected element of change to stop me from learning and growing personally and professionally. Everything happens for a reason.

You see, sometimes we're confronted with unexpected challenges (economic downturn and now the COVID-19 Pandemic), just like we face in the game of chess. At any given moment, you may find yourself trapped or frozen, not knowing what to do next. For many, fear plays a huge factor in contributing to and spreading a position of self-paralysis.

Yet, I'm so grateful I stayed focused and relied on my chess-playing skills to help me get through these unexpected tough times. I strongly believe because I am an avid chess player, I was able to analyze my problems with more logical clarity and make better decisions going forward.

Think about this . . . change is a funny thing that happens to us. Sometimes change can come from a position of complacency or as a result of a motivating circumstance. For me, change came very quickly and unexpectedly. This experience forced me to sit still and seriously reevaluate myself at a much deeper and higher intellectual level than ever before.

I deliberately persevered and was totally committed to my vision for my new goals for success and faced my curiosities of the unknown.

Proudly, in 2014, I launched SHESS Global Alliance, LLC and have been fervently teaching women in business basic chess tactics and how to transfer those chess-playing skills into their real-life situations for future business success.

As the Creative Founder & CEO at SHESS Global Alliance, I provide small business consulting services to entrepreneurs, inventors, and startup businesses throughout the United States.

More particularly, as a small business consultant for the New Jersey Small Business Development Center at Rutgers-Newark, I teach Executive Problem-Solving Tools & Tactics for Entrepreneurs, From Ordinary to Remarkable Leadership, First Steps to Entrepreneurship, and the Small Business Guide to Intellectual Property at local New Jersey universities.

In addition, I proudly teach life skills and chess to inmates and community-based clients at a corrections and rehabilitation center in New Jersey.

My message is clear. You do not have to be a chess grandmaster to take advantage of chess. Of course, this prestigious title is not easily attained, but for the rest of us, playing chess for fun is a great way to help develop our intellectual abilities and learn to think, plan, and react to things more effectively.

Checkmate Moves for Business Startups further reinforces my recommendation for you to play chess for fun and take advantage of its rewards and benefits. This book is meant to motivate and guide you to pursue your dream to start a business with insightful recommendations on how to proceed. I have basically combined a self-help, startup business guide for women in business, with a chess twist—how to elevate yourself from a Pawn status in life to a SHESS Queen in business.

I inspire you to adopt a powerful mindset through my Master SHESS Ideology and understand how the essential transformation, From Pawn to SHESS Queen theory, can help you succeed in life and business.

I welcome you to join me in taking a chance to learn chess and begin your SHESS journey of self-empowerment and accomplishment.

In SHESS, your game of life, the SHESS Queen is a metaphor which describes a successful woman who emerges from a perception of a weak position afraid to make decisions. She is not concerned about what others think of her.

This book will help you develop your endgame SHESS strategies for success. To be honest with you, I struggled at first with the notion women in business would not be interested in learning to play chess because they would be bored, intimidated, or just too busy in their lives. But my personal SHESS journey helped me to realize playing chess is not about winning or losing but daring to learn something new and using the tactical skills necessary to be successful in all that I do.

In my line of work in small business consulting, I have successfully counseled hundreds of female clients on what to consider and how to start up their businesses. I discovered throughout many of these counseling sessions that there is a common thread of fear of the unknown and a lack of confidence in their abilities.

Why do women block themselves from reaching their dreams of entrepreneurship and relentlessly wait for the approval of others before starting their own businesses? Why are women constantly scrutinized and labeled "bitches" for being aggressive just because they vocalize their opinions in society and the workplace? I believe this perception paralyzes women in more ways than one.

It is no secret that a woman who is intelligent and strong-minded is feared because she represents change and independence. Remember, knowledge is power. The more a woman is educated and professionally established, the more she is feared. Think about it. An accomplished, smart, and confident woman represents a financially secure woman who does not need to rely on anyone but herself to survive. Intimidation of a woman's success can also be another factor that plays into the fear of others.

Subsequently, instead of forging ahead with determination and resiliency, women sabotage their own successes, including personal and professional growth. Perhaps they believe they are not worthy or are undeserving of success. Some women even believe they should hold themselves back intentionally from being too successful because their significant other may get upset or feel resentful towards them. This kind of insecure mindset is dangerous! You should be with someone who accepts you for who you are and appreciates what you bring to the relationship.

In my opinion, success is attainable by anyone in life and business despite opponents and obstacles. You have to find a way to deal with all the challenges that can arise at any given time. Yes, mistakes are made, but it is the learned lessons inherent in those mistakes that matter most.

Chess has helped me to confidently confront and handle my own issues in life and business. Chess has taught me to always develop a backup plan and stand ready in the event something does not work out. Chess enabled me to understand how change can occur in a split second, and my focus on a particular matter is vital, while anticipating my opponent's next move without fear. Chess has also provided me with the confidence to make a move regardless of the outcome because I have carefully thought it through and will dare to take a chance on my decision.

Fear is a strange emotion, however. It will paralyze you and prevent you from accomplishing your goals. My advice is to let others' opinion of you be your go-to motivator for success. Take the negative and turn it into a positive. Learn something new (like playing chess) and be flexible about change.

I can confidently say playing chess will help you gain more logical clarity in your decision-making process just like it helped me. You may ask, "Is it possible to enhance and develop your cognitive abilities and learn smart strategies to become a better thinker and problem solver in life and business?" I say absolutely!

A SHESS Queen does not make any excuses for her victories. She is a woman with a powerful and resilient mindset! She is fearless! She is independent! She is successful!

INTRODUCTION

"SHESS" is a creative play on two words: "she" for female and "chess" for the game. Together these words represent "your game of life."

—WENDY OLIVERAS, AUTHOR

T HE ENORMOUSLY POPULAR NETFLIX series, "The Queen's Gambit," about a young girl living in an orphanage in the 1950's who reveals an astonishing talent for chess, has many lessons to learn as we watch her on her journey to adulthood to become one of the world's great chess masters. Her name is Beth Harmon, and she represents an intelligent strong female that faces many obstacles in life to find her place in the world, much like so many of us today and especially women who are balancing family and business.

As a successful small business consultant and avid chess player, I wrote this book to inspire women in business to take an interest in playing chess, learn smart tactics for success, and become equipped to fearlessly start their own businesses.

Women too often paralyze themselves because they fear the unknown and failure. Although fears are understandable and natural, my intention is to help prepare you to face unexpected challenges in life with confidence and to encourage you to start the business you've always wanted to without those fears.

I instinctively rely on my chess-playing skills to keep me focused and determined in my daily activities and business challenges. For this reason, I encourage and challenge you to learn to play chess so you too can gain an edge on your competition and develop smart tactical moves for future success in life and business just as I have.

Let's consider despite the surge of high technology, science, and innovation, women in business have attained many great and creative accomplishments. Yet, women still face barriers to earn equal pay to men and continue to struggle to be equally acknowledged and accepted professionally.

Women continue to lag behind men in business, including the professional world of chess which is another reason I was driven to write this book. This phenomenon should come as no surprise to anyone because women have had to work twice as hard to prove their abilities and roles in society and business.

In the professional world of chess, however, it is estimated less than 14% of members of the United States Chess Federation (USCF) are female and compete professionally worldwide. This is a very low percentage of professional female chess members. The truth is that male chess players are given more credibility and attention globally than female chess players. I never understood this.

Perhaps women do not want to take time to learn chess. Maybe women find it boring or have no desire to compete professionally because they are intimidated by the game and their male opponents. The fact is the journey of becoming a chess grandmaster takes real dedication, years of practice, and huge sacrifices.

Regardless, this undeserving perception is clearly unfair to those few female chess grandmasters who have dedicated most of their childhood and early adult life to professional study and mastering this fascinating board game.

So, I wonder with much curiosity why women in general ignore the great benefits and rewards chess affords them. I advocate for women of all ages and backgrounds to learn to play chess for fun and ignore the societal perception women are weak and intellectually incapable of becoming good or even great chess players.

This is why I have dedicated my efforts to demystify the basics of chess for women in business and teach them how to play while revealing the inherent analogies that exists in this intellectual game. The great news is you no longer have to fear chess because I am happy to simplify the game for you.

In spite of the underrepresentation of female chess players within today's competitive chess world, I would like to highlight the fact that women have actually contributed a key part in the development of the modern chess game.

Did you know throughout history women played a vital role in the development of feminine rule (aka the "Queen") on the chess board? As a matter of fact, for five hundred years, the chess game existed without the Queen.

The Queen was not always considered the most powerful piece on the board. Although the history of chess is unclear, it is believed chess originated in India around 600 CE and all of the pieces were male.

When chess began to spread to Europe around 1000 CE, the chess Queen began to appear on the board. The Queen at that time was considered one of the weakest pieces and was only allowed to move diagonally one square at a time.

It wasn't until the end of the fifteenth century that the Queen's powers were improved from its weak status to a more powerful and challenging position.

In her book entitled "Birth of the Chess Queen: A History," author Marilyn Yalom emphasizes that women have played a very crucial role in the development of the Queen's powers. In particular, Yalom references three strong historical women, Queen Eleanor of Aquitaine, Queen Isabela I of Castille, and Catherine the Great, Empress of Russia.

I want to share with you brief histories of these strong monarchs so you can appreciate the significance their contributions in ruling their respective countries made throughout Europe. I respect how each Queen successfully reigned during their time in history despite the obstacles and struggles they endured during their respective eras.

Queen Eleanor of Aquitaine

(1122–April 1, 1204)

Eleanor of Aquitaine was queen consort of France (1137–1152) and England (1154–1189) and the duchess of Aquitaine in her own right (1137–1204). She was one of the most powerful and influential figures of the Middle Ages. She inherited a massive estate at the age of fifteen, which made her the most sought-after bride of her generation. She would eventually become the queen of France, the queen of England, and lead a crusade to the Holy Land.

Queen Isabella I of Castille

(April 22, 1451–November 26, 1504)

She was ruling queen of Castile and León from 1474 and, through marriage, Queen of Aragon from 1479. She reigned over a united Spain together with her husband Ferdinand II of Aragon.

Queen Isabella I ruled during a time of war when ruling queens were rare. For example, women who inherited a throne were expected to turn their power over to their husbands and simply become their companions in life.

She changed her role in life from pawn to a powerful queen and used her power to influence politics throughout fifteenth century Europe. She also influenced the military by taking charge of strategy and tactical planning of war campaigns.

Some of Queen Isabella I's successes as her determination and struggle to claim her right to the throne, taking charge in reorganizing the governmental system, bringing crime to the lowest it had been in many years, and relieving the kingdom of huge debt that her brother had left behind. History also teaches us that she was best known as the woman who funded Christopher Columbus's first expedition across the Atlantic Ocean.

Catherine the Great

(May 2, 1729–November 17, 1796)

Catherine II, aka Catherine the Great, was Empress of Russia from 1762 until 1796. She was Russia's longest-ruling female leader. She came to power following a takeover funded by the British embassy that overthrew her husband and second cousin, Peter III. She was actually known for her scandalous affairs rather than for general state affairs, but she still managed to help expand Russia's empire.

Nevertheless, Catherine the Great was regarded as a socially open-minded ruler. She even corresponded over her life-time with one of the greatest French philosophers and writers, Voltaire (November 21, 1694–May 30, 1778). She was also known as a devoted supporter of the arts and opened the Hermitage Museum during her reign as part of her personal art collection. As a result of her ruling influence, Russians also adopted western European philosophies and culture.

Summary

Thanks to these strong female monarchs, the chess Queen as we know of today is the most powerful piece on the board! Many sacrifices were made and countless daring chances were taken to be recognized as powerful female rulers whose countries were typically ruled by men. They each successfully contributed to the success of their states and its people and influenced the transition of the weak Queen to the most powerful piece on the chess board today. What great and interesting facts to learn!

Regardless of the powerful symbol the Queen represents on the chess board, however, the unfortunate reality is female chess players are still frequently considered by their male opponents as weak.

I have experienced being told by a male opponent that my move was a cute one and then I would hear a giggle. I am not sure if the giggle stems from nervousness or fear of losing, but those types of comments and reactions only inspire me to play harder and smarter.

This is my empowerment message to you. You are not just a mother, daughter, sister, girlfriend, wife, or entrepreneur, but OWNER of your mind and OWNER of your individual ability to develop newfound strengths.

You have the choice to develop your intellectual capabilities and dare to take risks without fear of the unknown, failure, or even success. You have the capability to make mistakes and learn from them as well. By acknowledging and accepting your weaknesses, you have gifted yourself the permission to begin a self-empowerment journey in which to attain boundless rewards through self-awareness and personal growth.

The key is to take your time and grow from within first. By learning to take advantage of the game of chess, and having fun in the process, you have sparked a commitment to yourself to make your first powerful move towards your future success!

Change doesn't come easy and certainly not on its own. Change can only begin with a willingness to change. Are you flexible about learning new things? If you are, then allow me the opportunity to empower you through basic chess strategies. All that is required of you is to believe you are a powerful woman in the making and embrace motivation to fulfill something empty inside of you. Again, I ask you do you have a dream of starting a business despite all the challenges and obstacles you face daily?

Remember, as women, we were once considered weak, just like Pawns in chess, but we can develop our intellectual abilities and learn to make smart moves in our game of life.

The tide has changed but you need to do the work. Only we have the power to transform ourselves from perceived weak Pawn women to successful SHESS Queens in all we do. A Pawn piece never moves backwards on the chess board and neither should you in life!

My love and respect for chess is real! I also love teaching women in business how to play and how to transfer those invaluable chess strategies from the board to real life and business.

Don't be intimidated to enter my fun world of SHESS where you get to play your game of life your way! There's no winning or losing ... but play chess for fun, dare to take risks, and learn from your mistakes on and off the board, and keep it moving just like those strong female monarchs did so very long ago.

PART 1

ANALOGIES INHERENT IN CHESS, LIFE, AND BUSINESS

D ID YOU KNOW CHESS, life, and business have many commonalities that tie them together in a very unique way? In fact, did you know chess tactics are directly implemented in strategies related to education, politics, sports, everyday life, and business?

Tactics which are used on the chess board are likewise successful transferrable tools you can use in your daily life and startup business and development. Once learned, these tactical tools can also be used as an influence to help build confidence, make better decisions, set and accomplish goals, and solve problems with logical clarity.

Your task to complete: I have described below twenty-one key analogies inherent in chess, life, and business. As you read through each analogy, I want you to analyze and identify the ones you directly connect with either in life or business.

I then want you to choose six analogies which are most relatable to specific scenarios in your personal life or business goals. I've provided you with several blank pages for you to fill out at the end of this chapter, so please consider the following questions.

- What's on your mind?

- What challenges are you currently facing?

- Do you recognize any obvious or subtle commonalities between these six analogies?

- What else?

- How would you go about implementing a positive change in your pursuit of life or business goals?

- What is the most useful thing you learned today?

Once you begin to think in this way and recognize patterns, you will be surprised as to how many of these analogies are consistent and perhaps deceptive in your marriage, relationships, workplace, career, and goals you set for yourself, including making the bold move to start a business.

The most important thing to remember in completing this task is to use your feedback at any time to help you feel better about yourself and gain more confidence in setting and accomplishing your goals.

ANALOGY 1: Three Chess Stages and Three Business Phases

The game of chess has three main stages, including (i) the open game; (ii) the middle game; and (iii) the endgame.

The **open game** in chess represents the beginning of the game, your first moves, development of your pieces, and strategies you use to try and control the center of the board. At this early stage of the game, you begin your tactics and plan to deploy an attack.

The **middle game** in chess represents the sacrifices you make while exchanging and losing pieces. Note that a sacrifice is considered giving up a piece that has a higher value for a piece that has a lower value, e.g., sacrificing your Queen (nine points) for a Bishop (three points). This is not considered an even exchange. Sometimes, however, you can sacrifice a more powerful piece for a weaker piece depending on your next moves and your opponent's anticipated reaction to those moves.

The **end game** in chess represents the final stage or ending of the game. Here, few pieces are left on the board and you make your final moves to capture your opponent's King to win the game.

Similarly, there are three analogous phases in business, including (i) the **open phase**; (ii) the **middle phase**; and (iii) the **end phase**.

Every action or decision you make leads to an eventual and final outcome. But to successfully achieve your end phase result, the best tactic to implement is to have a final outcome in mind so the goal you have set becomes more attainable.

In other words, when you set a goal, there are three phases involved, such as the **open phase**, which represents the idea of the goal, the **middle phase**, which represents what you will do to achieve the goal, and the **end phase**, which represents the final result of the goal based on the moves you have taken. Did you analyze the phases for the goal, and did you succeed in accomplishing that goal?

As a matter of fact, have you ever heard the question "What is your endgame?" This metaphor represents the final phase of an extended process or course of events. You should be able to answer this question if you have set a goal and have envisioned what the end result should be.

For instance, by developing an endgame or end phase strategy for your startup business, you have planned smart moves in advance towards your future success. Remember, it's difficult to see the endgame of a goal if you can't imagine its future outcome.

ANALOGY 2: You Are Everyone's Pawn

This common metaphor "You are everyone's Pawn" or "You were a Pawn in that game" means you have been duped or used for someone else's purpose or benefit.

The Pawn piece in chess is considered the weakest piece, but it is the only piece which can be promoted to something of increased value.

Being considered everyone's Pawn has a negative connotation to it. You need to recognize when and if this is happening to you because being a leader requires being able to lead by example. Don't allow yourself to be pegged as a puppet in anyone's game.

In business, you must prevent yourself from being a Pawn at all times. You have worked too hard to get to where you are, so stay vigilant, observant, and determined to set and accomplish your goals regardless of what others think!

ANALOGY 3: From Pawn to SHESS Queen Theory

From Pawn to SHESS Queen Theory is an integral analogy and empowerment message tied into this book for every woman in business whether you are starting one or have an existing business.

A Pawn in chess is considered weak and worth one point, but it is the only piece in the game that has a special move to promote itself to a Queen, which is the most powerful piece on the board and worth nine points.

In SHESS, your game of life, every female born into the world is considered a Pawn in life. Although she may be viewed as weak, she too has a special move to promote herself to a SHESS Queen in life and business if she chooses. She accomplishes this self-promotion—From Pawn to SHESS Queen—by believing in herself, staying focused, facing fears, being proactive, making positive changes, and committing to smart decisions without looking back.

Think about the fact that women are restricted in movements and roles in society and business just as Pawn pieces are restricted in their movements and roles on the chess board.

A Pawn piece can promote itself to a Queen piece if it lands on a square at the extreme opposite end of the chess board. Since the Queen is the most powerful piece, this Pawn promotion, known as "Queening," would be the most logical to make.

Conversely, Pawns in life are women who also have special abilities, skills, and capabilities to promote themselves to a Queen status in life or business. So, "Queening" yourself from Pawn status to a powerful and confident Queen is a great special move you grant yourself for success.

This analogy is too important to ignore because it sparks the motivation you need to develop a more powerful and fearless mindset. Therefore, only you can promote yourself to something better!

ANALOGY 4: Respect for Your Opponent

Chess teaches you to respect your opponent. Before you start a game, you typically shake hands. After the game, and regardless of who wins or not, you shake hands again. While playing chess, respect is shown to the opponent by not talking, making sounds, or causing any physical distractions.

In business, you should also respect your opponent, whether it is an individual or competitor in your marketplace. I would even go as far as saying that you should respect your opponent at the start of a meeting or a networking event. You should at the very least acknowledge their presence and not allow anyone to intimidate you. So, move forward with confidence and determination. Awareness of your opponent, maintaining integrity, and having respect for others are key tactics for your overall success.

ANALOGY 5: Staying Vigilant and Alert

When you play chess, you must stay vigilant and alert at all times, especially observing what your opponent is doing on the board. If you don't stay vigilant and alert, you may put your pieces in danger of being captured. You want to anticipate your opponent's next move and make sure you develop a backup plan to protect each piece as much as possible so you don't sacrifice one of your pieces for something worth far less.

The same concept of staying vigilant and alert applies to your life circumstances and business dealings as well. You must stay vigilant and observant with regard to whom you allow in your personal life, whom you choose as a partner, and what vendors you do business with to avoid mistakes, deceit, or fraud. This may sound a bit extreme or paranoid, but the reality is staying vigilant and alert at all times can help save you from committing unnecessary mistakes in life or business.

ANALOGY 6: Controlling the Center

As mentioned in ANALOGY 1 above, during the open stage of a chess game, another very important tactic is to try and control the center of the board as quickly as you can. This is typically done with the use of Pawns and Knights. So, controlling the center means you have positioned and developed your chess pieces on the board and can threaten your opponent from the center and diagonally while simultaneously protecting your pieces.

In life and business, the strategy of "controlling the center" means you have to position yourself in such a way by making the right moves, controlling your emotions, and daring to make decisions while moving forward despite opponents and challenges.

ANALOGY 7: Anticipation of Your Opponent's Next Move

When you analyze and anticipate your opponent's next move on the chess board you are using an inherent tactic which is also used in real life.

In other words, while "anticipating your opponent's next move," you are actually thinking ahead and organizing your thoughts to help make your next move in response thereto, and the formidable cycle continues from that first move. So, you move and then I move in response, and then you move in response, etc.

After your opponent makes a first move, ask yourself "Why did they move there?" "What or who is my opponent attacking?" The key is to analyze and develop the ability to foresee at least three to five moves or options in advance to help you avoid and prevent surprises. In order to do this, I recommend you first:

(a) recognize the threat

(b) identify your opponent(s)

(c) consider what your next moves or options will be as a result of your opponent's first move

(d) anticipate your opponent's next move as a result of your next move

(e) don't be afraid to make a decision—but make a move

One main challenge to face is identifying your opponent(s). In Part III, External Obstacles and Internal Resistors, I discuss in more detail the two main categories of opponents you may face in life and business. Each type of opponent brings its own individual challenges.

For example, **external obstacles** represent a person, place, or thing that, by intention or not, is doing something to prevent you from moving forward with accomplishing your goal.

Internal Resistors, however, stem from deep within you and reflect how you see and think of yourself. This type of opponent is very powerful because it can stifle your growth potential. A negative mindset combined with a lack of confidence will paralyze you from making sound decisions.

ANALOGY 8: Attack and Defend

In chess, "attack" means to make aggressive moves that will weaken your opponent's position on the board and "defend" represents protecting your pieces from your opponent's attack.

In life and business, the term "attack" represents aggressive strategic moves you make to prevent competitors in your marketplace or someone in your life from gaining an advantage over you.

In the same way, the term "defend" means to protect yourself, including what's most important to you in life and business, e.g., your marriage, family, home, and business entity.

ANALOGY 9: Pattern Recognition

Chess allows you the ability to recognize and memorize moves and tactical patterns that are played during the game. No two chess games are ever the same.

It is the same concept in life and business. Being able to identify and recognize patterns in your personal relationships, as well as in business dealings, is critical to avoid making or repeating mistakes.

For example, you may end up deeply hurt again if you fall in love with the wrong person even after you recognize the same negative patterns of behavior from a previous bad relationship. If you decide to stay in this abusive relationship anyway and don't fully analyze or make any smart moves to avoid this repetitive pattern, you have not learned from your mistake.

Likewise, in business if you recognize a negative pattern with a client who is notorious for making late payments or not paying at all for services rendered and you continue to do work for this client, you have just enabled a repetitive pattern and made a huge mistake. You are not recognizing a harmful pattern, and this will cost you in the end. So, don't do it.

Your best tactic is to stay focused, anticipate and recognize bad patterns as they occur so you can anticipate what's coming next and avoid these negative outcomes in the future.

It is very important for you to develop a more strategic game plan when handling matters in business, especially those mistakes that are going to cost you money in the long run. I recommend you build better relationships with business partners and reliable vendors. Remember, better tactical decisions help to create better outcomes in the long run.

ANALOGY 10: Element of Change

While playing chess, there is always a constant and random "element of change," which occurs throughout the game. It is an unexpected change or move you did not expect or anticipate at any given moment.

Let's say your opponent has just made a move on the board that has completely thrown you off your game. You now have to respond to that move and configure an entirely new strategy to protect your pieces from that unexpected attack.

In life and business, elements of change occur all the time as well. Consider you have set certain goals for yourself and work hard towards achieving them. All of a sudden, "an element of change" occurs, and you are now distracted and cannot focus on a defensive strategy because you did not anticipate this move from your opponent. So, what do you do?

My best advice is to carefully think, plan, and then react to the situation. Consider the element of change as an immediate warning. Remember, never make decisions based on emotions. However, you must now do something or react differently than initially planned. Regardless of what you do, this element of change will affect the outcome of your next move directly or indirectly.

Therefore, you can either do nothing, make a change, or plan a more aggressive move to help get you back on track. Whatever you decide to do, don't be afraid to make a decision. Otherwise, you remain stuck in that unexpected element of change, paving the way for no growth, no development, and no accomplishment. Learn to analyze problems and structure a game plan because every move you make affects every outcome.

ANALOGY 11: Twelve Lessons Chess Teaches You About Losing

Generally, the word "losing" means being deprived of or ceasing to have or retaining something, including failing to win in a sport or game. The fact is chess represents an intellectual and logical game which mimics a battle of war between two minds. A winner emerges with a strong sense of victory, and a loser may walk away feeling upset and inadequate.

Naturally, the great feeling of winning boosts self-confidence and morale. The lessons inherent in losing in chess, facing life challenges, and handling business dilemmas are quite similar and relevant for success.

Whether you win or lose, playing chess reinforces a sense of confidence in your abilities. The ultimate lesson in losing is to accept the loss with grace and dignity, and to learn from your mistakes.

Analyzing your opponent's next moves, and your strategic responses thereto, are essential tools to help build determination and resiliency. Chess subliminally emphasizes losing as another stepping stone towards achievement. In other words, without mistakes on or off the chess board, there cannot be a paved way towards success. Only you can determine what works for you and what does not.

Chess also helps you to focus and build your mind, which is necessary in all facets of life and business. For instance, if you lose at a game of chess, it simply means you should work harder to improve your game, practice more, and learn from the mistakes you have made for future games.

In life, losing at something or not achieving a particular goal means you cannot give up. It is important for you to assess what went wrong so improvements can be made. Obviously, if you ignore your mistakes and continue to ignore possibilities, then it is important to acknowledge that more work still needs to be done.

Similarly, in business, losing can be analogous to not closing a deal, losing a major client, or losing customers due to a competitor's aggressive tactics in your marketplace. However, is it possible to lose at a game of chess or anything else and still be able to walk away feeling empowered and motivated by the loss? Absolutely!

The following is a list of twelve lessons chess teaches you about losing at something in life or business.

1. You are unique and have special capabilities and abilities.

2. Respect your opponent and lose with grace and dignity.

3. Nothing is perfect. Keep trying and give your best.

4. If something does not work out, create a new plan.

5. Stay focused. Concentrate and anticipate new challenges ahead.

6. Don't give up on anything you strongly believe in.

7. Don't be afraid to set goals and make decisions and future moves.

8. Accept your strengths and weaknesses. Acknowledge there is room for improvement.

9. Never stop learning and adopting new strategies.

10. Be flexible. Enjoy and embrace change.

11. Do not ignore repetitive patterns.

12. It's okay to lose as long as you learn from your mistakes and don't dwell on it.

Regardless of the reasons for losing at something, pick yourself up, learn from it, and keep moving forward.

ANALOGY 12: Learning from Mistakes

In chess, mistakes occur more often than not. This is part of the learning process. It is inevitable. What matters most is how you handle defeat, including learning from your mistakes.

In life and business, the similarity is obvious. Mistakes are always going to happen, but it is up to you to identify them and learn from them as they occur. Keep in mind repetitive mistakes only hinder and prevent your full growth potential for success. Your best tactic is to accept your mistakes as they occur, learn from them, and then move on! But don't look back!

ANALOGY 13: Losing with Grace and Dignity

While playing chess, you are doing two things simultaneously, such as defending your King from capture and attacking your opponent to capture their King and win the game. However, despite all of your efforts to win the game, you have made many mistakes along the way and have lost to your opponent. It is only natural to feel disappointed and frustrated, but there is no need to stay upset with yourself.

On the contrary, learning from your mistakes played on the board and knowing that by continuing to try again, you can pick yourself up with grace and dignity. Chess is a thinking and strategic game and everyone has a different learning curve. Be patient with yourself!

In SHESS, your game of life, it is not a matter of winning or losing at something, but rather what smart moves you are making towards your own success.

In SHESS, you are also doing two things simultaneously, such as defending your "King," which metaphorically represents whatever is most important to you, e.g., your business entity or marriage, and responding to your opponent with intelligent tactics to help solve challenges.

Ask yourself "Have I identified and analyzed my opponent(s) in life or business?" "Am I focused and anticipating my opponent's next move and developing the right moves to accomplish my goals whether on a personal or professional level?"

The point is not to give up on yourself just because you did not get what you wanted at any given time. Be kind to yourself and be patient with the process of what you are working on and learn from the journey of your mistakes, but safeguard yourself in order to grow from that point forward.

ANALOGY 14: Analytical Reasoning and Logical Thinking

It is no secret most of us cannot solve our own problems. Most of us do not realize in order to solve our problems we need to use our analytical reasoning and logical thinking skills—exactly the skills used in chess, life, and business.

This is one main reason why playing chess helps you develop your cognitive abilities to face challenges and resolve problems with more logical clarity.

Analytical reasoning skills help you make decisions based on information provided, and logical thinking skills pertain to the process in which you use your mind to consider something carefully, reasonably, and logically. These skills go hand-in-hand in solving problems.

ANALOGY 15: Critical Thinking

Critical thinking relates to the actual thought process and your ability to raise questions, articulate responses, gather relevant information, and finally come up with conclusions and solutions to a problem. It is a fact that without critical thinking, it is impossible to develop tactics and combinations in chess, life, and business.

ANALOGY 16: Creative Thinking

This particular skill enables you to develop creative and imaginary ways to help solve problems. Keep in mind no chess game ever repeats itself, so creative thinking is crucial since it allows you the ability to be flexible while you develop new tactics and moves throughout the game.

This is exactly what occurs in real life and business too. Whether on a personal or professional level, being creative with your thinking process, daring to take chances, and being fearlessly diligent in facing challenges will help you to solve problems whether anticipated or not.

ANALOGY 17: Confidence Building

As you learn to play chess, you begin to gain confidence in your overall abilities. Memorizing how each piece moves, their point values, and developing strategies and tactics towards winning are key. I know whenever I win a game of chess, I feel so happy and confident in my abilities.

This is also true in setting and accomplishing goals in life and business. The more goals you accomplish, the more confidence you build to help make better decisions. It's a natural transition towards self-empowerment, believing in yourself, and learning to take risks.

ANALOGY 18: Sacrifice

In chess, a "sacrifice" is considered losing, exchanging, or giving up a piece of higher value for an opponent's lower valued piece. Sometimes you have no choice, and you are forced to make decisions either way. Let's say you give up your Queen, which is worth nine points, in exchange for your opponent's Pawn, which is worth one point. This is called a sacrifice. Note this sacrifice can be considered a good strategy depending on the situation. Remember, if you must lose a piece, try and get something for it if you can.

It is the same way in life and business. A sacrifice can also occur when you give up something of higher value in exchange for something worth far less. It is an important and hard lesson to learn when you sacrifice something for another thing worth much less or nothing at all. Only you know what risks you want to take, but recognize what you are willing to sacrifice and why.

Stay alert and on top of your game when you make decisions about sacrifices. Most importantly, knowing the value of something important to you is vital and knowing what and when to sacrifice it is equally as important for your future victory.

ANALOGY 19: Stalemate

In chess, a "stalemate" occurs when the player whose turn it is to move is not in check but has no other option to make a move. When stalemate occurs, the game ends as a draw and there is no winner.

In life, a stalemate can also occur when you find yourself in a difficult situation and have reached an impasse or a point where neither you nor another person gain or lose something.

For example, if you know someone who has a serious addiction, and you have exhausted all measures to help that person change for the better. You are in a stalemate because that person does not have a true willingness to change for the better, and you gave it your all to help.

In business, however, a stalemate can occur between competing companies, colleagues, or coworkers who are confronted with a challenging situation. Therefore, they cannot move forward from a position of stalemate, and the relationship is no longer seen as acceptable by either party.

ANALOGY 20: Perpetual Check

In chess, if you check your opponent's King repeatedly, it is considered a perpetual check. More specifically, if you use the same three moves in trying to check your opponent's King, it is considered a stalemate or draw. No one wins. A perpetual check is typically used by the weaker side to avoid losing the game.

Similarly, in life or business, a perpetual check can also occur and result in a stalemate or draw when you keep repeating the same mistake over and over again and there is no improvement.

ANALOGY 21: Checkmate!

In chess, "checkmate" occurs when your King is put in check and you have no option to remove the threat of capture. Checkmate results in your opponent winning the game because your King was captured and vice versa—you win the game because you put your opponent's King in checkmate.

It is very common to hear people use "checkmate" in conversations to signify you either lost at something, have no other move left, or you made all the right moves and now you won at something. Another example is the title of this book, "Checkmate Moves for Business Startups," which means you have made the smart move to start your own business and use this book as your guide.

In summary, although the above list of analogies inherent in chess, life, and business is not necessarily exhaustive, it offers you a great way to recognize the challenges that are present in your life. The analogies can also be useful as a guide for you to apply them positively in facing life dilemmas and entrepreneurial aspirations.

By recognizing these common analogies and creating your own list for comparison, you learn to strategize your next moves with more determination and less fear, despite mistakes made along the way. You can always expect to do your best at something even if results are not what you hoped for and that's okay too. But never give up!

Go to a quiet spot and take your time really considering these twenty-one analogies and choose six that resonate with you the most.

YOUR TASK – Select six analogies that resonate with you the most. Consider how you can use each one to view your position in your personal and professional life. After you analyze each one, do you understand what your next moves should be to set and accomplish goals?

_____

_____

_____

_____

_____

_____

_____

_____

_____

_____

_____

_____

_____

_____

_____

_____

_____

_____

_____

_____

_____

PART 2

WOMEN IN BUSINESS
AND THE MASTER SHESS
IDEOLOGY

B ELIEVE IT OR NOT, chess mirrors your personal and professional relationships. It provides you with an exceptional opportunity to develop self-reflection, self-commitment, and self-determination to face fears, take risks, and make mistakes.

One of the most important lessons you will learn from playing chess is that despite your failures on the board, you learn to continue to move forward with resiliency and confidence in your endless pursuits of accomplishments. This is an invaluable reward chess gifts you and shouldn't be overlooked.

As a result of being an avid chess player, as well as my experiences as a small business owner of two companies, I learned that losing something is okay as long as I learn from my mistakes and the experience. I learned how to develop successful strategies to face my opponents and obstacles in life and business with confidence and resiliency despite my disappointments, faults, and bad decisions.

Consequently, I developed the Master SHESS Ideology to provide you with an effective road map from self-empowerment to a more developed and powerful mindset for leadership and achievement—just as playing chess has helped me in my life and business success.

The **Master SHESS Ideology** represents your emotional intelligence, which consists of five main components:

1. The **"S"** in SHESS represents your personal journey in "**SELF-EMPOWERMENT.**" This component has four sub-categories, which are crucial for understanding yourself and being brutally honest about what you will and will not accept in life. There must be a true willingness to change something about yourself or else self-empowerment will not be effective. There are too many obstacles and naysayers in the world. Ignore the outside noise and focus on your inner voice and intuition, which carries far more internal power and credence. You know yourself better than anyone so don't allow anyone to manipulate you into thinking otherwise.

   (i) **Self-Awareness**: The first step to encouraging self-empowerment is to be self-aware of who you are and know what is important to you. What are your strengths and weaknesses? What are your personal boundaries? What are your true fears? Not knowing or understanding these things about yourself means you need to dig deeper, so start digging!

   (ii) **Self-Acceptance**: The second step to determining self-empowerment is to accept yourself just as you are at this very moment. Know that nothing and no one is perfect, and that is just fine. But you must be open to change and accept there is always room for improvement. Once you begin to honestly accept yourself as you are, you can then allow yourself to fully commit to change or improve something about yourself. Be open and dare to take a chance.

(iii) **Self-Improvement**: The third step to achieving self-empowerment is to create a strategic plan of action and next moves to invigorate self-improvement. Are you seeking a job promotion? Do you feel you need more education or training? Do you want to start a business? Focus and know what you want, set a goal, and then start planning for it.

(iv) **Positive Self-Talk**: The fourth and most crucial part of attaining self-empowerment is learning the art of self-love and always being kind to yourself. Positive self-talk means you need to commit to reprogramming the way you think. Do you like the person you are? Are you angry at yourself for past mistakes or bad decisions? Always remember that having a good relationship with yourself first is a dynamic and powerful smart move. If you say downgrading things about yourself such as "I'm so dumb!" then how can you progress? By always thinking and saying positive things about yourself, despite how you feel at any given moment, is key. Don't be afraid to laugh out loud when you make a mistake or make a wrong decision. Don't be unfair and impatient with yourself. Instead, learn to be patient with your truth and accept all of your flaws, but stay determined to make necessary adjustments when necessary. Keep telling yourself every day that you are important, good, smart, capable, and yes, beautiful! Tell yourself hard work pays off in the end and no one is perfect. Just do you! Love yourself each and every day and stay open to learning new things.

2. The **"H"** in SHESS represents your **"HONOR SYSTEM."** This component has three sub-categories, which are essential for developing and implementing strong principles:

(i) **Integrity**: In order to have integrity, you have to be honest and truthful with yourself. Accept the good and the bad and make changes where necessary and appropriate. Integrity is that subtle thing about yourself that never changes, even when you are sitting alone and no one is watching or with others in a room. Your Honor System depends on you having integrity. Always be a woman of your word! Be honest about what works for you and be clear about what you will and will not allow. Set boundaries with clarification but don't stifle your growth.

(ii) **Empathy**: Your Honor System is also contingent upon having empathy for others because having understanding, sympathy, and compassion for others is what makes you special, honorable, and a good leader. Being responsive to someone else's need is a great unselfish act. Besides, helping others also makes you feel good about yourself and helps you gain confidence in your abilities too.

(iii) **Self-Respect**: Your body is your vessel, but your mind is the vital engine, which runs it with or without you being aware. Regardless, your body and mind should be in harmony and must be respected at all times. If you don't respect your body, then don't expect others to respect it either. If you don't take steps to learn new things or stimulate inner curiosity about the world, you may be missing out on some great new adventures. You are solely responsible for taking care of your mind and body because it is the only one you have been given. Enjoy healthy eating, exercising, and living in the moment, but don't forget to have fun. Take time to nurture yourself, sit still, and be very kind to yourself.

3. The **"E"** in SHESS represents **"ENGAGEMENT."** This component has four sub-categories and specifically pertains to gaining confidence, setting goals, and developing tactics to make smarter decisions. It is important to anticipate problems before they occur versus

sitting around dwelling in misery and depression and reacting to a negative outcome after the fact.

(i) **Proactive versus Reactive**: A proactive tactic relies upon your ability to anticipate issues before they occur. In being proactive, you focus on preventing, avoiding, or eliminating problems before they happen. On the other hand, a reactive tactic is relative to your response to events after they have occurred. The major difference between these two tactics is your perspective. How you think, react to things, and assess actions and events is key.

(ii) **Set and Accomplish Goals**: It's a difficult task to set a goal if you don't have an idea of what you would like to do or accomplish. Only you know yourself and what is best for you. If your passion and dream is to have your own business, then go for it.

(iii) **Be Open to Change**: Don't let fear stop you. Fear paralyzes your creativity, thought process, and ingenuity. Making excuses and being unwilling to take a chance at learning something new can be an easy way out. What is the worst thing that could happen if you try something new? You can walk away knowing you at least tried. This is an accomplishment in itself too. Be daring and explore new things by allowing your creative side to wake up and have fun in the process.

(iv) **Learn from Mistakes and Avoid Repetition**: It is sad to see when people continue to make the same mistakes over and over again, but never learn from them. Don't be that girl! Stop beating yourself up about things that happened in the past. Accept your mistakes and keep moving forward because those mistakes are actually successful lessons learned too.

4. The second "**S**" in SHESS represents "**SMART MOVES FROM PAWN TO SHESS QUEEN.**" This component has three sub-categories, which relate to problem-solving strategies to help you create a plan of action to succeed in accomplishing your goals:

   (i) **Think.** When you are faced with a dilemma, think about what just occurred and try to understand its motive or intention. Emotions tend to get the best of us, and the worst decisions and mistakes are made out of emotions. So, be clear about your needs and set boundaries whenever necessary.

   (ii) **Plan.** Once you analyze and understand the problem at hand, you must then start planning your next move by considering various options and solutions available to you and anticipate what your opponent may do in response to your move and so on and so forth.

   (iii) **React.** Once the problem is clear to you and you have analyzed all of your options, it's time to make a decision, but stick to a decision. Don't be afraid to react and make a move!

5. The last "**S**" in SHESS represents "**SUCCESS.**" This component also has three sub-categories, which pertain to attributes acquired for the benefit of others so the cycle of success can continue:

   (i) **Help others.** In times of trouble, it is a great feeling when you help others in need or perform a simple act of kindness for no special reason. Helping others helps you feel better about yourself. Humanity for humanity.

   (ii) **Respect others.** Treat others the way you want to be treated. Respect for others is crucial for a thriving society and community to get through life's struggles together in many respects, including business settings.

(iii) **Mentor others**. So, you have accomplished your goals in life and business and now it's time to mentor those less fortunate or in need of guidance from someone they can trust. This is equally a very gratifying feeling when you have mentored another girl or woman to not make the same mistakes you have made and teach them how to stay positive. Motivate other women towards a path of success.

The above components and subcategories of the Master SHESS Ideology may seem overwhelming, but if you analyze them carefully, it all comes down to how you think, plan, and react to things in life.

The reality is self-empowerment only works when you have a willingness to change and a commitment to improve something about yourself. There's no magic potion you can take to fix negative things, but you can change the way you think and react to things in a more positive way.

The assumption you need to be born an entrepreneur to be successful is not true and not a prerequisite. The truth is that starting up a business is challenging. If you decide to start a business, be serious about your commitment to successfully execute and grow the business idea.

Keep in mind passion and really caring about what you do for others will guide you along the long journey ahead. Some people say that you do not need passion to have a successful business. For some this may be true, but for others passion is what drives their motivation and thus, a desire to keep going despite challenges.

How you personally face failures in life is also key if you want to succeed. Stay strong, focused, and maintain the tenacity needed to keep moving forward. Never stop learning and asking questions. Don't be afraid of taking chances or taking risks because failure and rejection don't define who you are as a woman or business owner. So, try harder to limit your risks by staying ahead of your competition.

The assumption you need lots of money to start a business is also not true. Although having startup capital helps, it is a myth that investors are ready to break down your door to give it to you. There are many other options available to you, but you have to do the leg work and investigate the best choice.

Always remember we do not grow when things are going well, but grow when things have gone wrong and we have learned from mistakes. This is an integral part of inner growth and rising from within first and developing the tenacity and dedication required for future success.

PART 3:

IDENTIFYING AND OBSERVING OPPONENTS IN LIFE AND BUSINESS

H AVING THE ABILITY TO listen to and trust your gut instincts is a great skill. But it is a personal skill most women do not develop either because they live in fear, ignore their feelings, stay complacent, hope for the better, or remain in a constant denial mode.

Truthfully, many women do not listen to their intuition and end up in very bad situations, facing circumstances that could have been avoided had they merely listened to their gut instincts. This is why it is so important for you to learn to not only listen to your gut feelings, but identify opponents in your life and business so you can help mitigate at least some unnecessary negative or damaging outcomes.

There's no perfect science to this, however, a strong sense of awareness that something is wrong or does not feel right is key. When you do sense something is off, you should be prepared to analyze it and plan to make a move without fear, to avoid a bad outcome.

Similarly, in chess and in life you basically know who your opponent is for the most part, but you still need to focus and trust your gut instincts as you recognize patterns on the chess board and in your personal and business relationships. This has been and continues to be an increasingly common occurrence and repetitive pattern with women in general.

Let's analyze this further. If you feel something doesn't feel right, why are you going forward anyway? By not trusting yourself, you open the door to negativity or a potential disaster. If lack of confidence, low self-esteem, or even fear to speak up for yourself is a problem for you, then you need to make some changes now and fast to improve this way of thinking and behavior.

Your thoughts and opinions matter! You do a disservice to your integrity and well-being if you stay quiet, hold in your feelings, and do not speak your mind when something is wrong or being unfairly done to you. This self-defeating passiveness needs to change! You need to stop being afraid of making decisions and start making smarter moves to improve something in your life or business.

A SHESS Queen thinks like a strategic chess player and recognizes her opponents in life and business. She faces her situations fearlessly and with determination regardless of the outcome.

More specifically, with regard to the concept of identifying opponents in your personal life, this may involve a family member, friend, neighbor, or significant other.

In contrast, identifying opponents in business, such as a direct competitor in your marketplace, also requires clarity, focus, and intuition-building skills. You may or may not personally know someone in business who is trying to weaken your position in your industry, company, or field. But look out for those invalidators who are persons intent on smiling to your face and all the while trying to take your place behind your back. Yes, you read that correctly! By invalidating your abilities and capabilities through others, invalidators tactfully control a situation that is prevalent in life and business. Stay vigilant and observant!

In SHESS, your game of life, there are two main categories of opponents you may face in life or business, e.g., **"External Obstacles"** and **"Internal Resistors."** What is important to note is both categories of opponents exist in some form or another to prevent you, directly or indirectly, from setting and accomplishing your goals. Sometimes these opponents mask themselves as allies, but in reality, they exist to deter or stop you from doing something positive or succeeding, e.g., invalidators.

It is your responsibility to stay vigilant and identify your opponent(s) in each category of life and business. You need to learn the hard lesson that making decisions based on emotions is never a smart move. Instead, a smarter tactic is to learn to make better decisions based on logical clarity and focus in order to avoid negative consequences. I have taken the liberty of highlighting each category of opponents in life and business below:

1. **EXTERNAL OBSTACLES** are considered those opponents in life and business which relate to a:

    • Person, place, or thing;

    • Spouse, romantic partner, family, friend, neighbor, stranger;

    • Competitor in your marketplace, business partner, colleague, coworker; or

    • Lack of capital or funding.

I want you to close your eyes for a moment and think about someone or something in your life that is making you feel uneasy or uncomfortable right now. Are you paying attention and listening to your gut instincts? What is your gut revealing to you? Regardless of what it is, something just doesn't feel right and you can't put a finger on it. Well, it is up to you to analyze the situation and try to understand why it is happening and what it is threatening.

Likewise, when you are playing chess and your opponent makes a move, you need to analyze why your opponent made that move and what piece is being threatened. It is very easy to get distracted; that's why it is important for you to stay focused and pay attention. The point is by not doing something to prevent your opponent from stopping you from accomplishing your goal, you will not succeed at something.

Remember, your external obstacles come in the form of a person, place, or thing. With regard to a person, this could be anyone you know and possibly someone you don't know. It could even be a group of people. Regardless, stay alert and observe what is occurring around you. Be patient and think things through, develop a plan of action, and then execute your next move. Take a chance, take a risk, but make a move!

With regard to an external obstacle in business, however, this opponent can be a direct competitor in your marketplace, a business partner, a colleague, supervisor, or a coworker, depending on the circumstance. As a business owner, the one thing you must always protect is your business entity, which is synonymous to a "King" in SHESS, your game of life— just like you must protect your King in chess from being captured by your opponent.

Sometimes an external obstacle can also present itself in the form of a lack of capital or funding to grow your business. This obstacle can be readily dealt with depending on your circumstances and other contributing factors, which may play a part as well. Again, analyze what needs to be done, when, and how. If you are overspending in general, then maybe you need to cut back on expenses and start budgeting yourself accordingly. There are always solutions to problems; it's a matter of thinking them through, planning ahead, and then executing your next moves for successful outcomes.

2. **INTERNAL RESISTORS** are considered those obstacles which stem from deep within you. Internal resistors are those elements which directly pertain to:

- How you generally perceive and react to things;

- Negative thinking, negative self-talk, self-imposed fear, procrastination, low self-esteem, self-doubt;

- Too much confidence and arrogance, which can also sabotage your successes; or

- An injury, illness, abuse, addiction, tragedy, death, or loss.

In considering how external obstacles and internal resistors affect our thinking and overall well-being, I believe identifying each category can help to develop smart strategies to protect you from irreparable harm and prevent emotional pain and unfortunate failure.

For example, how you generally perceive and react to things can determine the outcome of any situation. Obviously, overreacting and allowing emotions to cloud your strategies to make better decisions will have a negative result. However, by taking a minute to reflect and think things through without fear or anger, your decision might have a more attainable result. It's up to you to know when and how to react to those unexpected elements of change that occur in your life or business. In chess, this element of change occurs constantly, and it is in your best interest to identify and face the change.

Negative thinking and negative self-talk are definitely not in a SHESS Queen's mindset nor something I advocate in this book. The moment you articulate into the universe the words *I can't*, *I'm not able to*, or *I won't*, you can't expect a positive outcome. You have just sabotaged yourself from succeeding at something. Totally unnecessary!

Instead, try consistently switching negative words into positive and motivating words such as *I can, I will*, and *I'm willing to try something new*!

A SHESS Queen avoids negative thinking because she is confident in her abilities. She would rather take a chance at something than not try at all. A SHESS Queen is curious, fearless, and relentless in her pursuit of a positive and successful life.

What about self-imposed fear, procrastination, low self-esteem, and self-doubt? Do these elements of internal resistors define who you are as a woman? Your dream of entrepreneurship and independent financial security has just gone out the window because of these negative self-imposed internal resistors. Try and catch yourself when and if you find yourself thinking negatively. As soon as you recognize this negative way of thinking, immediately switch to a more positive tone and take a deep breath.

If you resist yourself, you leave no room for growth and development. Instead, try gifting yourself the wonderful opportunity to learn new things and become more flexible and patient about change. Fear will always exist. At least try to acknowledge your fears and take the necessary steps to prevent paralyzing yourself from accomplishing your goals. You waste time and energy living with a negative mindset. Change is good, so embrace it.

Other elements of internal resistors that can exist include injury, illness, abuse, addiction, tragedy, death, or loss. These internal resistors can also directly affect your personal and professional progress. Listen, I get it, and I have been there myself. Life is difficult and things can change from one moment to the next, but it is how you see yourself, think, and approach challenges or unfortunate situations that matters the most. Things that are out of your control can definitely stop you completely from making the right decisions. However, I strongly urge you to be patient, analyze your situation carefully, and don't give up on hope, faith, and determination.

On the other hand, abuse is a whole other challenge to deal with. Whether you realize it or not, it is easier to fall prey to an abusive situation or relationship than it is to stand up for what you believe in and have the strength to walk away. Regardless, you must be able to identify what is best for you and dare to walk away and never look back if it is not a good or safe situation for you. Every problem has a solution. Don't accept something negative in your life as the only option available to you. Carefully think it through and sort out the alternatives for a better result and long-term happiness.

Lastly, with regard to addiction, you always have a choice. Either you realize drugs and/or alcohol are destroying your life or you don't. Focus on how your family, friends, coworkers, or employees are reacting to you. This is your personal choice to make, but you need to learn to fight the right battles that affect you directly and those that can stifle your attempts to reach goals for success.

I realize many women fear rejection, failure, and even success. But if you don't become aware of and identify your internal resistors, you can't expect positive results from your decisions or actions. Having emotional intelligence is key to your ultimate success in all you do. You can't live a good life being upset with others or blaming others if you do not progress at something. This is your life! Live it to the fullest but don't waste it masking your true feelings. Living is feeling, and life is what you make out of it.

YOUR TASK – Select one external obstacle in your life that is standing in your way for growth. After you have identified that obstacle, select one internal resistor you feel gets in your way that you need to work on.

_____

_____

_____

_____

_____

_____

_____

PART 4

ENDGAME VISIONARY STRATEGIES TO SET AND ACCOMPLISH GOALS

D**O YOU GENERALLY FIND** it difficult to set goals and then fail at accomplishing them? How does that make you feel? Choosing goals and achieving them is easier said than done, right? Let's say you pick a goal you are super excited about. You feel ready to devote your time and energy to it, but you find it hard to come up with ways to start and accomplish that goal. Well, you are not alone.

Maybe you didn't want to complete that goal bad enough from the start or perhaps you allowed someone or something to get in your way? There are so many excuses for not starting or completing a goal such as procrastination, which is a quick way to become lazy and get stuck because you didn't try hard enough.

The core issue here stems not so much in setting a particular goal but in envisioning its outcome and planning strategic moves to begin and complete that goal.

You need a vision for that goal!

When you set a goal for yourself, imagine what that completed goal might look like in the future, i.e., your endgame visionary strategy. See yourself in that successful role and get happy about it. Ask yourself what do you want to ultimately accomplish with regard to that one goal? I firmly believe what really helps in setting and achieving goals is having a vision with strong conviction to succeed, focus, mental organization, and advance planning.

I would like to use the goal of starting your own business as the primary example for implementing your endgame visionary strategies for success. My helpful tips outlined below will guide you in the right direction without sacrificing your self-confidence.

- Have a vision set of being your own boss.

- Close your eyes. Feel the success while imagining the rewards and benefits of accomplishing the goal to start your own business.

- Focus on what is most important to you and your family.

- Mentally organize what next moves you need to make to get you jumpstarted and headed towards the finish line.

- Continue to plan in advance by anticipating potential obstacles, which will help mitigate unfortunate consequences from mistakes.

Remember, there's nothing you can't do if you apply yourself, stay focused, remain resilient, and be fearlessly determined to accomplish your goals.

It would be remiss of me if I didn't mention that one key principle in chess is to not make careless Pawn moves. Pawns cannot move backward—only forward. Making wrong decisions does not insulate you from the consequences. Understanding the situation at hand and identifying the circumstances surrounding the decision-making process is most crucial.

A SHESS Queen understands she is going to be faced with challenges and obstacles, but does not allow anything to hold her back. This is certainly *not* an option for you either.

Nothing can stop you now!

As I mentioned earlier in Part 2, and based on my Master SHESS Ideology, which focuses on the importance of emotional intelligence, you are guided in the direction of self-awareness and self-empowerment. Believing in your abilities, forgiving yourself for past mistakes, and learning from bad decisions can help to turn negative results into positive future outcomes.

By focusing and implementing your endgame visionary strategies, you will begin to embark on a determined pattern of setting goals you want to achieve and understanding the moves you will need to make to successfully accomplish those goals despite obstacles or opponents you may confront.

YOUR TASK – Describe a personal goal and then a professional goal you would love to set and accomplish. For each goal, implement your endgame visionary strategies. What do you envision for each goal?

_____

_____

_____

_____

_____

_____

_____

PART 5

SMART TACTICS TO HELP YOU SOLVE PROBLEMS

M OST PEOPLE CAN'T SOLVE their own problems because they basically don't know how to resolve them. The majority of these people end up in difficult and regrettable situations that could have been avoided from the beginning.

Recognizing you have a problem or challenge is the first step; analyzing and understanding what is involved is the second step; and setting a plan to solve the problem is the third step. Note these three smart tactics are used while playing chess as well.

To further help you learn to think through and solve problems, I highly recommend you implement a strategic planning technique called the "SWOT Analysis," which consists of your strengths, weaknesses, opportunities, and threats.

Your SWOT Analysis

SOURCE	HELPFUL	HARMFUL
Internal	Strengths	Weaknesses
(attributes of the individual or organization)		
External	Opportunities	Threats
(attributes of the environment)		

Keep in mind the purpose of your SWOT Analysis is to help you pinpoint sources that are helpful or harmful to your success. For example, **internal** sources are attributes such as your strengths (which are helpful) and weaknesses (which can be harmful). **External** attributes are considered those characteristics of the environment such as opportunities (which are also helpful) and threats (which can also be harmful).

So, how can you begin to use your SWOT Analysis to help you start a business. Contemplate if there are any particular problems, situations, or circumstances affecting your goal to start the business. Do you understand the financial projections needed to start the business? Is your vision for starting and building the business on point and focused? Let's dig deeper.

Strengths

Begin with considering the strengths in your analysis, which are considered the characteristics of the business that give your company an edge in the same marketplace and in contrast to your direct competitors. When you conduct the strengths analysis of the business, you will need to:

- highlight the industry you are in as compared to other industries; and

- describe how your business would be making the best use of its resources, services, or exact products.

Weaknesses

Consider weaknesses, which are characteristics of the business that are considered disadvantages as compared to your competitors. It is very important for you to identify what improvements are needed in the business no matter how unimportant you think they may be.

In contrast, consider external sources, which are those opportunities or possible threats that can also represent elements not derived from the business but still rely on the result. In order to maintain control over positive or negative outcomes or achievements, you will need to analyze those external sources carefully as well.

Opportunities

Having a clear sense of what is working and what is not helps the business ebb and flow through its growing pains. For example, opportunities are those positive external possibilities that can improve your business and achieve a better consequence. Here you should list ways in which to predict how your business could grow now and in the future. Be creative!

Threats

Threats, however, are those characteristics of your business that may have a negative influence on future growth potential and create issues, which may prevent your projected outcome and expectations. Even outside forces could affect the business, such as less customer demand in your marketplace, lack of technology, lack of legal protections, economic downturn, and even a Pandemic.

The importance of analyzing problems

The truth is bad decisions and mistakes are usually made as a result of a lack of understanding, lack of a strategic plan, anger, sadness, or fear. The consequences of decisions that are not properly analyzed are most regrettable and result in unhappy consequences. So, try your best to analyze problems first and then develop a tactical plan of action to help you solve those problems with more logical clarity.

In life, just as in business, unexpected situations occur all of the time. I like to refer to these unexpected circumstances as "elements of change," which not only occur on the chess board, but in real life and business dealings too.

What is vital to know is how you approach problems and how you react to them when they do arise. When you are faced with a problem, do you stop to analyze what has just occurred? Do you then consider various options to help you resolve that issue? Or do you just ignore and pretend the problem will go away on its own if you don't do anything—denial? Oh, and by the way, procrastination is another way to avoid your problems, which will also harm you equally as much as the bad decisions you make.

I suppose it's easier to blame others for your mistakes and actions instead of accepting total responsibility for your decisions. But at the end of the day, you are an adult who is responsible and accountable for each and every decision you make.

The fact is there are many external obstacles to deal with, including all of the daily pressures to compete with others in business and be successful, general life distractions, technology, the internet, and the speed of life. You owe it to yourself to be more self-aware and self-accepting and know what you are capable of.

How to develop a strategy

Your Task – Complete your answers below for each question as best as you can.

Where are you right now?

- Think about how you got here. What has worked for you and what hasn't?

_____

_____

_____

_____

_____

_____

_____

_____

_____

What do you need to change?

- Compare where you are right now in your life as opposed to where you want to be in the future.

- Think about what is holding you back.

- What do you need to stop doing that prevents you from progressing?

- What do you need to start doing instead, to get what you want?

_____

_____

_____

_____

_____

_____

_____

_____

How do you determine your progress?

- Don't get upset with yourself and don't get hung up on negativity. Stay focused!

- What progress have you made to help bring your strategy and vision to realization?

_____

_____

_____

_____

_____

_____

_____

_____

_____

Where do you want to go?

- Think positive while prioritizing what is important to you.

- Imagine life without obstacles.

- What truly motivates you?

- What is your reality and what are your expectations?

_____

_____

_____

What do you need to do to obtain your success?

- Be patient with yourself and the process while developing your strategy.

- Do you need to get help from others?

- What help or support do you need?

The essentials of being and living without fear

Finally, I recommend the following tips to help you feel better about yourself and encourage you to make better decisions without fear.

- **Be alive and present in this current moment.** Stop and smell the roses, as they say. Feel, smell, and touch everything in your life as best you can and appreciate what you have right now because tomorrow is not promised.

- **Be honest with yourself.** If you don't know who you are and what you are capable of then you are missing so many wonderful opportunities. Being self-aware and self-accepting are key self-empowerment moves for your overall success.

- **Be determined to adapt and change.** Nothing and no one is perfect but making the decision to change for the better is a good start and will help you gain momentum much easier.

- **Be clear about what you will and will not accept in life and business.** Communication with clarity regarding your boundaries are important to develop so trust for others and self-confidence can be built on a strong foundation.

- **Be committed to your decisions and don't look back.** After you have efficiently analyzed a problem carefully and considered all options, don't be afraid to make an informed decision. Stay committed to the decision you make. Don't look back.

In retrospect, taking the time needed to face issues and learning to solve problems while being true to yourself and others is a win-win for all—especially for those affected by your focused decision-making process and smart tactical moves.

PART 6

STARTUP CHECKLIST FOR THE SHESS QUEEN IN BUSINESS

I WANT TO FURTHER EMPOWER and motivate you on your quest to becoming a small business owner and becoming financially independent.

But before we begin, I recommend you to take a few deep breaths and concentrate on erasing any negative thoughts, doubts, fears, or anxieties from your mind. I encourage you to ignore what others say and focus on what matters to you most.

"I can do this! I will do this!"

The following is your personal Startup Checklist for the SHESS Queen in Business. I have organized the checklist into seven major categories. I want you to review and consider each category carefully.

CATEGORY 1
Evaluate your startup idea and opportunity

I advise you to make a list of your business ideas and match them to your strengths and interests. If you are having trouble narrowing down what is a good idea for you, then research businesses that are having success in today's marketplace.

Ideas

Is your business idea helping to solve a particular problem? Who is your target customer audience and market you wish to pursue? Perhaps talk to potential customers about your business idea to see if it is of value to them and worth pursuing.

To further help you evaluate your startup opportunity, I want you to think about what type of business you want to open. What inspired your idea for the business? Does your business idea actually help solve a problem in your community or the world? Do you have a particular skill or talent you can teach others and make a living out of it? Do you have experience and knowledge of the field and industry you are choosing to start a business in? Or do you have a passion for a hobby and desire to turn it into a prosperous business?

What is important to evaluate at this early stage of your business idea is the reason why you desire to start a business in the first place.

Do you know what you contribute and bring to the table as the business owner? Have you considered whether your business will provide a product or a service? Will you require a brick-and-mortar (physical location) or is the startup an e-commerce (web retail) business? Note there are various challenges you face in opening a storefront business versus an online business. Having a storefront business requires more money to cover the overhead expenses such as rent, utilities, furniture, and supplies as opposed to an e-commerce business, which requires minimal overhead costs such as web hosting monthly fees.

Financing

Have you analyzed if you need capital and if so, how much do you need to fund your startup endeavors? Have you determined a financial projection for how long this funding will last? If you don't know how much you need and why, this could lead you into lots of headaches later on.

Take the time to research various lenders and take advantage of your local small business development (SBA) center for capital resources and guidance on how to obtain a small business loan. Review the SBA's site at www.sba.gov for more funding resources and information.

Additionally, determine if the business should be run on a part-time or full-time basis. Many women work full-time jobs and start their home-based businesses on a part-time basis. Once you determine the business is growing and providing increased revenue that exceeds what you bring home from a full-time job, then maybe it's time for a new strategy for your next move. I don't, however, recommend you leave your financial security and benefits from your full-time position to start the business, however. Statistically, businesses fail within the first two years due to lack of preparation and funding. So, be patient.

Support from others

Lastly, ensure you have a good support system at home. Once you've made the decision to start a business and begin the process, explain to your family members that in order for this to take off, you will need to focus on the time, energy, and countless late nights it will take to get the business up and running. Ask them to be patient with you. Tell them to understand that your startup goals and sacrifices are intended to help the family financially as well. Don't forget to explain many sacrifices will also need to be made on their behalf as well.

CATEGORY 2
Commit to the startup process

Once you have decided on a solid business idea whether it is a product or service, you need to commit to the next steps necessary to understand what is required and what needs to be done next.

Business Plan

I advise you to create a business plan that includes financial projections and describes your costs and projected sales to determine if your money brings you a profit. Again, I recommend you contact your local SBA office for further help on creating a business plan.

CATEGORY 3
Moves to get you started

1. **Did you create and research the business name for the company?** Make sure to Google the name of the company to see if it is not already taken. If it is available, then register the domain name and start securing social media profiles for the company. You can also check on the www.sba.gov site to ensure the company name is available.

2. **Apply for a Federal Employer Identification Number ("FEIN") with the Internal Revenue Service ("IRS") at www.irs.gov.** Think of the FEIN as synonymous to your social security number, but for the business. Depending on the type of business you have, make sure to research whether you require local or state business licenses as well. You can also contact your local township for more guidance on licensing requirements.

3. **Next, and most importantly, decide on the legal business entity structure and then incorporate the business.** Below I have briefly

described the legal entity status options and respective pros and cons for each, including Sole Proprietorship, General Partnership, Limited Partnership, Limited Liability Corporation ("LLC"), Limited Liability Partnership ("LLP"), "S" Corporation, and "C" Corporation.

Sole Proprietorship

A Sole Proprietorship is the simplest form of a business entity but is *not* recommended.

PROS

→ You have complete control.

→ No corporate tax payments.

→ You can decide to sell or transfer the business easily.

→ Minimal costs to form.

→ Not many formal business requirements.

→ You can pass the business down to your heirs.

CONS

→ You are 100% personally liable for debts and obligations.

→ You are responsible for liabilities incurred as a result of acts committed by employees.

→ You are responsible for all decisions and responsibilities.

→ Investors are not usually interested.

General Partnership

A General Partnership allows you to have two or more partners owning the business. However, each partner has unlimited liability for the debts of the business. This is *not* a recommended choice either.

PROS	CONS
➤ Ease in which it can be formed.	➤ Each partner risks being personally liable for the debts and liabilities of the business.
➤ Little or no statutory formalities.	

Limited Partnership

A Limited Partnership allows you to have one or more "General Partners" and one or more "Limited Partners." Note that General Partners operate the business, while the Limited Partners tend to be passive investors. This type of Limited Partnership is often used for operating real estate, restaurants, a venture capital, or hedge fund.

PROS	CONS
➤ Limited Partners (as long as they are not actively participating in the management of the company) have limited liability.	➤ General Partners still have unlimited liability (unless a General Partner formed its own separate company, that General Partner would still be subject to all debts, as well as be personally liable, even for some of the debts of the business).
➤ It's a separate legal entity, unlike a General Partnership.	
➤ Can open up a bank account, conduct business, and own property in its own name and not in any one individual name.	

Limited Liability Corporation

A Limited Liability Corporation ("LLC") is a more popular choice for most entrepreneurs. An LLC has owners, called members, and has limited liability for the actions of the business. An LLC basically combines the best features of both corporations and partnerships.

One good example of an LLC is a company that exclusively uses the internet as a source of income, as well as brick-and-mortar companies. Note that banks or insurance companies cannot form an LLC.

PROS	CONS
➤ Company has a tax pass-through which means the company does not pay taxes on net profits.	➤ Depending on the state, an LLC will have to pay a franchise tax (privilege of having limited liability). This fee varies per state and can be based on revenue versus a flat fee.
➤ Owners pay taxes on income from the business that is reported on their personal tax returns.	➤ Usually have higher legal fees since "S" and "C" corporations already have ready-made agreements.
➤ Have a more flexible taxation option. Owner can choose a tax option as a Sole Proprietor, partnership, S-Corp, or a C-Corp.	➤ Difficult to obtain capital from investors because most investors are uncomfortable investing in a company that does not have shareholders or a non-incorporated business.
➤ Neither shareholders nor owners are held responsible for debts unless a member specifically signs an agreement assuming liability for a debt.	

Limited Liability Partnership

A Limited Liability Partnership ("LLP") is a corporation that offers its partners limited liability as per the amount of their investment into the company. Owners are protected from paying accumulated debts to their business. Both partners may control the day-to-day operations of the business. Note that many states limit the formation of an LLP to architects, lawyers, healthcare professionals, and accountants.

PROS	CONS
⇾ Owners can protect their personal wealth. (If the business falls into debt and the owners have no liability protection, then creditors can sue you for your business and personal money.)	⇾ Revenue or property gain made to or by the LLP is directly owned by the LLP and not the individual partners or co-owners. So, in order to allow for returns or individual benefits from these contributions to the LLP, specific agreements have to be written and signed.
⇾ Allows more than one partner to work for the business.	
⇾ No need for standard corporate practices, i.e., having annual meetings on the company's financial statements and business status.	

"S" Corporation

An "S" Corporation is a small business corporation that has been elected for S Corporation status through the IRS. The "S" comes from the Subchapter S of the IRS Code. Note this status allows the taxation of the company to be like a partnership or a sole proprietor instead of paying taxes based on a corporate structure.

An "S" Corporation can have no more than a hundred shareholders. Shareholders can be individuals, estates, or certain trusts.

PROS

→ Main tax advantage is there is no corporate tax. Profits and losses of the business pass through to owner's personal income tax. Similar to the LLC's tax pass-through, it allows owner to avoid being taxed twice.

→ Business can have reduced taxable gains when the business is sold. Something to consider as part of your retirement strategy.

→ Startup losses can be offset against owner's personal income.

→ Have some liability protection, but owner can be held personally liable for individual actions.

CONS

→ Only have one class of stock. Without different classes of stock, less control over the business and limitations on the stock value.

→ Venture capitalists are not interested and it's generally difficult to attract outside investors.

→ Although owner avoids corporate taxes, they still has to file a tax return every year.

→ Hold regular meetings and maintain company minutes.

"C" Corporation

Finally, a "C" Corporation, also known as a standard regular corporation. A "C" Corporation has a more complicated structure than an LLC. It is a corporation filed under Subchapter C status with the IRS.

It is legally independent from its owners and is not a personal tax liability for its owners. It also has a board of directors and shareholders.

PROS	CONS
➤ Main advantage is that the owners have no restrictions on ownership and are not personally responsible for the company's losses or debts.	➤ Costs to set up can be in the thousands of dollars, depending on how the company is set up.
➤ The investments made by the owners are their only financial risk.	➤ Since incomes are received by shareholders through dividends, which is how company profits are distributed, company can be taxed twice (double taxation).
➤ Depending on the owner's business income, a lower tax rate is possible.	➤ Are subjected to more government scrutiny due to complex tax rules, protection afforded to the owners from personal responsibility for debts, lawsuits, or the financial obligations of the business.
	➤ Must report annually to the state where they are incorporated.
	➤ Hold regular meetings, maintain company minutes, and issue stocks.
	➤ Names of corporate officers are made public.

4. Once you have decided on the legal entity status for your business, it's time to **start getting your website up and running**.

5. **Create your company's accounting plan and hire an accountant**, select an accounting system that works best for you, and a fiscal year, which is an accounting period of twelve months.

6. **Research, select, and decide which insurance policies** are best for your business, including professional liability, general liability, workers' compensation, or health insurance.

7. Go to the bank and open up a small business checking account and obtain a business credit card.

8. Start networking and getting your pre-marketing materials ready, such as business cards, brochures, and begin building your social media platforms. Most popular today are Linkedin, Facebook, Instagram, and Twitter.

CATEGORY 4
Do you need or have sufficient capital for the business?

There are several things to consider when ensuring you have sufficient funding for your startup efforts.

- Try and estimate how long it will take for your business to start having paying customers.

- At the very least, budget your personal living expenses for the first year and determine where this money will come from.

- How much capital will you need to launch the business? Project how long before you turn a profit.

- If, aside from seed funding efforts, including your own savings or money borrowed from family or friends, you determine you still need more capital and outside investors, then you should complete a business plan. This will certainly be required for small business loans and potential investors, e.g., venture capitalists or angel investors.

CATEGORY 5
Business plan considerations

It's no secret writing a business plan is a daunting challenge because there is so much involved in researching, organizing details, and incorporating complete financial projections. Of course, the SBA is a great resource to use because they offer help in writing your business.

If you are really ambitious and don't have the time to take an SBA workshop, then consider reviewing the book "Anatomy of a BUSINESS PLAN: The Step-by-Step Guide to Building a Business and Securing Your Company's Future (Small Business Strategies Series)" by Linda Pinson, author of the SBA Publication, "How to Write a Business Plan," 8th Edition.

As a further guide, below I have provided key sections of the business plan to help you at least begin the process of outlining one yourself.

1. It is strongly advised to write an **Executive Summary** of your business after the other six sections of the business plan have been completed. The Executive Summary is a brief outline of your company's purpose and goals.

2. Write the **Company Overview** of the business. This part includes basic information of the owner(s) and a summary of the management team, if applicable.

3. Write a **Product or Service Description** section, which describes your product(s) or service(s) and specify what problems they solve.

4. Prepare a **Market Analysis,** which describes your total market, including your target audience, specific industry segment needs, competitive offers currently available, and any trends that will affect your market analysis. Your market analysis section of the business plan is very important because it helps prove to potential lenders or investors that you have carefully studied and understand your industry and respective marketplace. It also helps to support an opportunity for any potential investments in your company.

5. You will need to describe an **Operating Plan** for the business, including your operating hours, number of employees, key suppliers and vendors, and any seasonal adjustments you might need to make.

6. At this point, you will also need to create a **Marketing and Sales Plan**, which includes your launch plan, pricing, customer leads, and how you will close new business dealings.

7. Lastly, you will need to build a **Financial Plan**, which illustrates a break-even analysis, a projected profit and loss statement, and projected cash flows.

If you have trouble finding the market and financial data needed to complete the Market Analysis and Financial Projections sections of the business plan, I recommend you contact your local business school library and obtain help with tips on how to obtain the appropriate data for these sections.

CATEGORY 6
Setting up the business to work

If you decide on a brick-and-mortar for your business, you should seek and secure a viable business location that provides your employees and customers with safety, easy access to public transportation, good parking, and handicap accessibility.

If you decide on a home office, be creative and design it with a pleasant ambiance and comfort zone by lessening distractions as much as possible.

If you will have employees, then you will need to know the profile of the employees and consider your staffing needs.

Now, if you decide on using independent contractors, then vet them carefully and have appropriate Independent Contractor Agreements drawn to protect yourself from unnecessary liability. Be sure to recruit, interview, hire, and train the best employees that fit your mission, vision, and culture for your business.

Ensure your business is staying competitive in your industry and marketplace by identifying and setting up the appropriate technology needed including, but not limited to:

- Point of Sale "POS" (in person or online),

- emails,

- telephones,

- Customer Relationship Management "CRM" system (to manage customer data),

- billing and payment systems.

Don't forget to protect your technology systems and secure your business information and customer data. With today's technological capabilities and cyber threats, consider investing in cyber security. Of course, you want to protect any trade secrets your company has that should not be shared publicly.

Depending upon the type of business you have, I recommend you always research and partner with the right vendors, distributors, and suppliers because establishing long-term relationships is key to your future growth.

CATEGORY 7
Congratulations! Market and launch the business

You're almost there! Hang in there with me! Regardless of the type of business you are starting, the following suggestions focus on marketing, branding, and launching your new business:

- Remember, your brand needs a great logo, a message that reflects your brand. Create a tagline your customers will connect with. I find connecting with customers emotionally is key. Develop and design specific brand templates for all your marketing materials and be consistent with your message and overall brand.

- Try and develop a thirty-second elevator pitch, which you can use in conversations with anyone, including potential clients or investors.

- Consider distributing or displaying shop signs, brochures, or banners for your marketing materials.

- Your online presence is just as important. Develop an effective digital marketing plan that includes your website, blogs, emails, and SEO strategies to direct traffic back to your website.

- If you have it in your budget, consider hiring a salesperson or a sales team to assist you with generating business leads.

- Announce your launch date via local or regional press releases.

- Organize your opening day and have fun with the entire process. Congratulations, SHESS Queen! You have put a lot of hard work and sweat into this one business venture, so enjoy your accomplishments to the fullest! You did it!

From a great idea to a booming business, it's a great adventure.

"Do or do not. There is no trying only do!"

—YODA

SPECIAL NOTES ON MARKETING AND BRANDING

By Lorraine Santoli, Former Marketing & PR Executive, The Walt Disney Company, and author of the book, "Inside the Disney Marketing Machine."

My twenty-two-year career with The Walt Disney Company under the tutelage of Michael Eisner provided me with an amazing education in marketing and branding. I learned from the cream of the crop and had the opportunity to engage with some of the most creative and talented executives in the entertainment industry. While my view of the importance of marketing and branding in business is from a "Mickey Mouse" point of view, the basics and fundamentals of utilizing these skills effectively cuts across all industry segments.

As Wendy Oliveras, the author of this book, explains, the game of chess has many similarities with the game of business, especially as it applies to women. Those who master the tactics, strategies, and approaches to each move they make across the business gameboard puts them in a stronger position to compete, just as thinking three or four steps ahead in the game of chess gives you an advantage against your opponent. And marketing and branding is key to that effort. After legally setting up your business as outlined in this book, begin to structure a marketing plan.

Today, as a marketing consultant, I am often shocked at how little attention marketing and branding gets from small business owners. For some reason, it is often given very short shrift in the big picture. This is a major mistake! As a person launching a new business by selling a product or providing a service, how can you possibly be successful if no one knows about what you're offering? That's what marketing is . . . your communication link to your target audience. According to The American Marketing Association (AMA), their official definition of marketing is the activity and process for creating, communicating, delivering, and exchanging offerings that have value for customers, clients, partners, and society at large. Marketing must always be an important part of your business plan. And the very first and most vital step in your marketing strategy is to define your target market. Who will be the key audience for your product or service?

Target marketing should be as specific as possible as to those demographics. The worst answer to the question, "Who are you targeting?" is "Everyone." You need to be precise. Is it women from 18-34 that are single or married, men from 35-49 who are white-collar workers or blue-collar workers, teens that use social media 4–8 hours a day? Break it down to your niche group. And what about the scope of your communications to your constituents? Is your reach going to local, regional, national, or international? These are all important foundational issues to help formulate your marketing strategy. The plan itself should be a fluid document that is flexible and can change as needed while it provides you with the path forward to communicate who and what your business is to potential users of your product or services.

Next comes the branding part of the marketing equation. What that means is creating a name for your business, along with a symbol or design (a logo) that identifies and differentiates your business or product from others that already exist in your genre. A tagline to your logo is key as well. The tagline needs to be unique and succinct, and one that captures the essence of your brand. Think about some of the world's most well-known brands and their visual icons and taglines—Coca-Cola, "It's the Real

Thing;" L'Oréal, "Because You're Worth It;" Nike, "Just Do It;" American Express Card, "Don't Leave Home Without It."

Developing your own brand strategy will give you a major edge in increasingly competitive markets. According to Entrepreneur magazine, "Simply put, your brand is your promise to your customer. It tells them what they can expect from your products and services, and it differentiates your offering from that of your competitors. Your brand is derived from who you are, who you want to be and who people perceive you to be." The finalized logo needs to be placed on all marketing collateral materials, from business cards to stationary, postcards, presentation folders, flyers, and most importantly, on a branded website and blog. All collateral must match and be consistent in style and colors.

Depending on your available budget, the plan might then be divided into three marketing arenas—Advertising, Promotions, and Publicity. This is where social media comes into play big time. Using social media networks like Facebook, LinkedIn, Twitter, Instagram, and so many more actually puts every small business on the same footing as a mega global corporation because the exposure is virtually free. No longer do you need to spend millions of dollars to promote your brand; just take to the internet, and get going. Here's a brief definition of my three tenets of getting the word out:

- **Advertising** is the attempt to influence the buying behavior of customers or clients with a persuasive selling message about products and/or services in ads that are paid for by your business. This is worthwhile but can be costly as ads must be designed, written, and placed in appropriate media to reach your target audience.

- **Promotions** are special events, contests, coupons, product samples, t-shirts, buttons, etc. Promotions can be more low cost than advertising but still require a financial investment.

- **Publicity** is using the news or business press to carry positive stories about your company or your products. It involves writing press releases, pitching stories about your product or service to media, posting to social media sites, writing a blog . . . essentially pushing out interesting and newsworthy information about your company. The most important thing about Publicity vs. Advertising and Promotions is that Publicity is FREE. Just get it out there yourself, and if it's newsworthy enough, media will pick it up, social followers will re-post it and their friends may do the same, word-of-mouth will push it forward, etc., etc. Importantly, because Publicity is not "paid-for advertising," the information will be considered more credible than an ad that anyone can buy. This factor actually makes the message more valuable. Consider how many photos and short videos go viral online reaching millions of people . . . at no cost to the person or company that posted them!

Let's take a closer look at just a few of the most popular social media platforms that can carry your marketing message to your constituents:

Facebook* - Facebook is a free social networking Web platform that promotes and facilitates interaction between friends, family, and colleagues. Create a Facebook page for your business and post to it daily with information, stories, photos, videos, etc. Let everyone you know and ask them to "like" your page. Facebook is the largest social network in the world. As of June 2019:

- Facebook reports an estimated **2.7 billion Monthly Active Users**.

- Facebook also says it has **1.6 billion Daily Active Users**.

- 88% of Facebook's user activity is from mobile devices.

- The average amount of time a user spends on Facebook every day is 58 minutes.

- There are over 300 million photos uploaded to Facebook every day.

- On average, five Facebook accounts are created every second.

- Approximately 30% of Facebook users are aged between 25 and 34 years.

- Facebook video is still in high demand, with approximately **8 billion video views per day**.

Source: Facebook Quarterly Reports

YouTube* - YouTube is the second ranked social media network where users can post videos about every imaginable topic. Consider starting your own YouTube channel to showcase your business. Currently, YouTube pulls in the following numbers:

- Has more than **1.9 billion logged-in visits every month**.

- **149 million people** log in to YouTube daily.

- The average duration of a YouTube visit is **40 minutes**.

- Viewers are spending an average of one hour per day watching YouTube videos.

- On average, **300 hours of video are uploaded every minute** on YouTube.

- There are over **5 billion video views each day**.

Source: YouTube Blog and Press Page

Instagram* - Instagram enables sharing of still photos and videos. Think the myriad ways to communicate your business messages via this source that is immensely popular and has some fascinating statistics:

- Instagram has over **1 billion monthly active users.**

- There are more than **600 million daily active users.**

- There are now **500 million daily Stories users.**

- Since its creation, more than **40 billion photos have been shared.**

- On average, **95 million photos are uploaded daily** on Instagram.

- There are approximately **4.2 billion likes per day**.

- Most Instagram users are between 18 to 29 years of age with **32% of Instagram users being college students.**

*Source: Instagram Press

Twitter* - Twitter is what's happening in the world and what people are talking about right now:

- Twitter has more than **330 million monthly active users** (MAU).

- There are **134 million daily active users** or at least that's how many "monetizable" daily active users there are, according to Twitter.

- Of their monthly active users, **68 million MAU are from the United States**.

- The number of **monthly active daily users from the US is 26 million**.

- Close to **460,000 new twitter accounts are registered every day.**

- Twitter users are posting **140 million tweets daily**; that adds up to a billion tweets in a week.

- Each twitter user has, on average, 208 followers.

- 550 million accounts are reported to have at least sent a tweet.

*Source: Twitter Earnings Reports

LinkedIn* - LinkedIn is a social networking site designed specifically for the business community:

- LinkedIn has over **560 million registered users**.

- It is estimated that LinkedIn has approximately **303 million monthly active users**.

- **5.3 million new accounts per month** are created on LinkedIn.

- There are over **30 million company pages**.

- The average visit duration is about **10 minutes**.

- Of all the users, 57% are male whereas 43% of the users are females.

*Source: LinkedIn "About" Page

While so much more can be said of marketing and branding, what has been presented in this chapter touches upon some of the most important keys to success when it comes to launching a new company for the SHESS inspired small woman business owner. It's the take-off point. How you creatively use these foundational marketing building blocks will determine how far you will fly. I'm betting after reading this entire book you will soar!

Your Task – Startup checklist – What is my business idea and what do I need to do to get jump started?

_____

_____

_____

_____

_____

_____

_____

_____

_____

_____

_____

_____

_____

_____

_____

_____

_____

_____

_____

_____

_____

_____

_____

_____

_____

_____

_____

_____

_____

PART 7

TOP 10 MISTAKES YOU MUST AVOID IN BUSINESS

A S FOR EVERY GOAL you set for yourself, there is always going to be room for mistakes. The dictionary's definition of mistake is "an error in action, calculation, opinion, or judgment caused by poor reasoning, carelessness, insufficient knowledge, etc.," including "a misunderstanding or misconception."

Learning from mistakes is what can help you to prevent further errors from occurring in the future. While life throws unexpected obstacles at us often, starting a business or growing an existing one is also very challenging. Things can change from one minute to the next. However, anticipating issues before they happen and being as prepared and organized as you can be will reduce future liability to you and your company.

Use your intuition

Have you ever felt like something is wrong or something doesn't feel right, yet you proceed forward anyway, and then realize you have just made a huge mistake? Perhaps you partnered with the wrong person to start the business and several months later you regret that decision for whatever reason.

Well, as I mentioned before, not using your intuition also occurs when you play chess. You are doubtful about making a particular move. You make the move anyway by ignoring your gut instincts. Now, suddenly, your opponent makes an unexpected move on the board and you realize you have just made a big mistake.

To help guide you in going forward, the following is my list of Top 10 Mistakes You Must Avoid in Business. Although there are other mistakes not mentioned, I created this list to focus on the ones that seem most common in startups.

Mistake No. 1:
Not believing in yourself or your dreams.

You block yourself if you are insecure and doubt yourself. A lack of self-confidence in your abilities can keep you trapped and feeling suffocated in your life and career.

Building self-confidence is part of taking risks because even if you fail at something, you help gain the confidence to try again and achieve personal and professional aspirations. No one is going to give you the confidence you need to believe in yourself. Only you can do that! By not believing in yourself, you definitely prevent yourself from being successful.

Below I have indicated a few suggestions to point you in the right direction to help build your self-confidence:

- **Try and promote a good positive attitude by being aware of your negative thoughts and refusing to allow those negative thoughts to overpower your positive ones.** It is equally as important to keep positive, trusting, and supportive people around you for moral support.

- **Be mindful of how you deal with your emotions.** It is never a good time to make major decisions based on emotions, so try and become comfortable with your fears, be patient with yourself and the process, and STOP comparing yourself to others! Each of us is entitled to our own life journey. Focus on recognizing and changing your own insecurities and bounce back from your mistakes.

- **Love and commit to self-care.** Not only does your attitude need to be positive, but you need to love yourself as you are and put good care into your appearance, eat well, and sleep well.

- **Set small, realistic, and attainable goals first and don't be afraid of taking risks while embracing the unknown.** DON'T be so hard on yourself either! Mistakes happen. It's the lessons learned from your mistakes that are vital for personal growth and development that matters most. I am a firm believer it is always better to try at something than not to try at all. A SHESS Queen in her game of life is not afraid to explore the unknown. She is a self-confident risktaker and has the determination to go for it.

Mistake No. 2:
Not conducting proper research.

Starting a business requires patience, extensive preparation, and research on your part. You may have a great business idea, but then you find out you made the mistake of not protecting yourself or the business from the beginning. If you do not conduct proper due diligence and research, you are headed for unnecessary liability and eventual losses.

It is so important for you to understand your marketplace, competitors, and target audience. Most businesses are now starting online and, depending on the product or service, the owners may decide they need a physical location. If this applies to you and you seek a location for the business then consider the following:

- Research the proximity from the store to public transportation.

- Make sure there is adequate parking for your customers.

- Check for high foot traffic.

- Determine how visible the store is to potential new clients.

- Project what the total anticipated financial costs will entail, such as rent, utilities, equipment, supplies, and anything else you need to run the business (you can include this data in your business plan to anticipate accurate financial expenditures).

Mistake No. 3:
Not planning beforehand and rushing to launch.

It is only natural to get excited about starting a business and the idea of being a business owner. But it is a big mistake to not plan ahead before rushing to launch the business. If you do not take out the time to carefully plan your next steps to build a strong foundation for the business, it will probably fail sooner rather than later. When a house is built, it requires a strong foundation, right? Well, it's the same concept for starting a new business—the foundation needs to be strong. Don't rush to launch the business and then realize soon thereafter that too many mistakes were made and you lost money unnecessarily.

Mistake 4:
Forming the business in the wrong legal status.

It is important for you to understand which type of legal status the business should be formed under. For instance, if you form your business as a sole proprietor, this means you will be solely and directly 100% responsible for any liability. In other words, if you get sued by a customer or vendor, you will be personally liable and could lose your home, car, and personal assets.

It is recommended you form the business as a Limited Liability Corporation ("LLC") instead to protect yourself from direct personal liability if the business gets sued. You can also speak to your accountant or CPA to discuss which legal status is best for you.

Mistake 5:
Not obtaining proper protections.

Depending on the type of business you have, don't forget to consider legal protections such as small business insurance. The most popular types of business insurance include professional liability/Errors & Omissions (E&O) or general liability.

You can and should also consider whether you need to obtain intellectual property protection to protect your patent idea, trademark and logo, or copyrights from being stolen, if applicable. I recommend you check out the United States Patent and Trademark Office website at www.uspto.gov to obtain more information about intellectual property requirements if you choose to go that route.

Not everyone is able to understand legalese and there comes a time when you will be presented with contracts. I recommend you consider hiring a corporate attorney to protect the legalities of your business as much as possible from unexpected or unfortunate losses.

A few common legal documents you may need or come across are Independent Contractor Agreements, Non-Disclosure Agreements, Operating Agreements, financial documents/loans, leases, client service agreements, product contracts, and vendor agreements. Regardless of the type of contract you need to sign, be smart about having it reviewed by an attorney to help lessen future losses to your business.

Mistake 6:
Choosing a bad business partner(s).

It is crucial for you to know who you are doing business with, especially if you add a legal equity partner. Ask yourself the following questions:

- How well do I know this person?

- What does this potential partner bring to the table?

- How can I leverage that individual's experience and knowledge into the business?

- Is this person of direct value to the future growth of the business?

- Can I trust this person and is there proven loyalty and commitment to me and the business?

Just as you should vet all vendors before going into business with them, you should also scrutinize any potential legal equity partner(s). My best recommendation is to be patient with this decision-making process because one wrong move can hinder the growth of the business or destroy it altogether. Remember, listen to your gut instinct and stay vigilant for potential red flags.

Mistake 7:
No strategy for branding, marketing, advertising, or sales.

Too often people start businesses and forget the importance of forming it with a brand in mind. The marketing and advertising tasks are also neglected, and the owner can't figure out why there are no sales. If you disregard building a brand for the business, including the name, logo, and message to your potential clientele, you will lose traction for growth.

Consider what resources you are using to market and advertise the new business? How will you grow the business and inform your potential clientele what you do and why you do it?

If you are not computer savvy and don't know where to start, a smart strategy is to consider hiring a marketing consultant who can help bridge the gap between what you lack and what is needed to help build your company brand and get more sales.

Mistake 8:
Quitting your full-time job before the business takes off.

If you are employed full-time, then I highly recommend you DO NOT QUIT your job until your business takes off. You want to be able to earn enough revenue to sustain yourself from that business income. Too many people have started businesses that failed and had quit their jobs within the first few months. Big mistake!

Mistake 9:
Not being cost-effective and spending too much too soon.

I can certainly appreciate that you are excited about your new business venture, but don't get crazy spending money above your projected budget. Don't start overspending on things you really don't need. Anticipate costs, research all expenditures, and compare vendors to assure you have made a good and cost-effective decision. This is a smart move!

Mistake 10.
Lack of networking with others.

There is a common saying, "You never know who you might meet." If you don't network with others, then you are missing out on great potential opportunities to help grow your business.

Staying home and being shy is not going to cut it. You are a business owner—a confident SHESS Queen—and you need to get out of your shell and make yourself more visible to others, whether in person or virtually. The key is to build long-term successful relationships with your peers, colleagues, and business partners for years to come. Sustainability in your marketplace is important for your business survival.

PART 8

BEST MOVES FOR YOUR
FUTURE SUCCESS

I T IS SO REWARDING for me to know you are reading this book with curiosity and determination to make positive changes in your life and finally start a business you can be proud of.

I am sure you have faced many challenges and bad situations in your life, but here you are still vibrant and alive, contemplating on how best to improve something about yourself. This is exciting!

I want to remind you that being an avid chess player for many years has honestly helped me to think, plan, and react to challenges with more logical clarity and build my self-confidence to make better decisions personally and professionally.

I have trained myself to be proactive versus reactive when facing whatever life throws at me, including confronting business dilemmas head on. I do my best to analyze a problem, come up with options for better solutions, and make a decision without fear of the unknown.

I have made a conscious commitment to myself that I will always remain flexible and open to learning new things. Fear will always exist, and how you confront fears matters most. Your mindset is a powerful tool. If you know you are afraid to take a chance at something and you fear the unknown, you may sadly miss out on some amazing opportunities. So, at least try!

For women in business, however, the challenges are much greater than they are for men because of the social and professional stigma tied to just being a woman. The unfortunate truth is that women business owners and women in high corporate positions still struggle to be on equal footing as men.

Are we to continue crawling under rocks when faced with resistance and not pursue our dreams of establishing our own businesses to gain financial independence? NO! On the contrary, we need to forge ahead, bravely facing the unknown and working hard on making smarter moves towards our future success!

I was inspired to create the metaphor "SHESS" because it truly represents "your game of life" and mine. SHESS is designed to empower you through basic chess strategies and inspire self-improvement. Wouldn't it be nice to learn how to build intellectual tools needed to make better decisions? I know you will also benefit from my Master SHESS Ideology and Pawn to SHESS Queen Theory just as I have all of these years.

So, without further ado, the following are my best empowerment moves for you to make for your future success:

→ BELIEVE IN YOURSELF

→ LEARN TO PLAY CHESS AND HAVE FUN

→ ADOPT THE MASTER SHESS IDEOLOGY

→ LEARN TO MAKE BETTER DECISIONS

→ DARE TO SET AND ACCOMPLISH GOALS

→ FACE YOUR OPPONENTS WITHOUT FEAR

→ EMBRACE CHANGE AND STAY FOCUSED

→ RESPECT, HELP, AND MENTOR OTHERS

Notwithstanding any and all of your life's challenges, don't let great opportunities pass you by simply because you are shy, afraid to make a change, or insecure to take a chance.

Think positive and believe in yourself first, and you will see good changes begin to happen. Don't listen to the naysayers, and focus on what matters to you most. Learn to play chess and have fun in the process!

Adopt the Master SHESS Ideology and stop procrastinating! Learn to make better decisions by analyzing your problems with more patience and resiliency. Stop being afraid to set and achieve goals. Believe me, once you succeed at one goal, you will be motivated to keep setting more. Face your opponents in life and business without fear. Get yourself unstuck! Embrace change and stay focused on what is important to you and fixate on your endgame visionary strategies.

Lastly, respect, help, and mentor other women in business, including girls in your family and community, to learn from the mistakes you have made and provide them with the nurturing support they need to succeed in their lives as well.

The days of elbowing each other are over ladies! It's time to embrace, empower, motivate, and join forces as humble, resilient, and successful SHESS Queens in our game of life and business! Time to celebrate! Where's the wine?

PART 9

LEARN TO PLAY CHESS
AND HAVE FUN!

I AM SO HAPPY YOU have chosen to learn to play chess! In playing chess, the beauty lies in developing skills, which help you learn to solve problems instead of learning solutions to problems. You begin to feel more confident in your abilities, learn to develop more creative and strategic tactics, and apply effective action plans to any life or business situation.

Chess is a positive motivator because it arouses self-motivation and builds confidence at any age. For instance, girls who are encouraged to play chess early in life develop self confidence in their abilities, team playing, patience, and respect for the game. They adapt and deal with new changes as they occur, develop leadership qualities, and learn to lose a game with grace and dignity.

These inherent lessons and improvement of life skills are beneficial for parents to appreciate and support. At the end of the day, if parents overlook the benefits that playing chess promotes in their children, they may be sending the wrong message. Chess builds their children's life skills and academic achievements. More particularly, if girls are taught to be afraid of the game and are led to believe they are not intelligent enough to play, then the wonderful opportunities and rewards gained in learning chess early in life are lost. Although it's never too late to learn to play chess, starting early in life is a great way to develop a young girl's math and science capabilities as well.

Let's start with chess basics

Chess has specific rules, which all players must learn. Since these chess rules may seem intimidating to a beginner, I have carefully provided a simple version of the basics.

To begin you will need a chess board and chess pieces. The chess board is an 8 X 8 grid (8 rows and 8 columns) with a total of 64 squares. The rows on a chess board are called ranks and the columns are called files. A chess board is always set up with a white square on your right.

There are two players in a game of chess. Each player starts with sixteen pieces in the same color, referred to as white and black. White moves first and a coin toss is often done to see who gets the white pieces. (It doesn't matter which color or ornamental design is used for the chess set as long as each side is distinguishable from the other, e.g., light and dark.) Each player will have one King, one Queen, two Rooks, two Bishops, two Knights, and eight Pawns.

If you touch a piece, you must move it. This is called the "touch move rule." If you cannot move the piece because it is illegal, then you can move another piece. If you need to touch a piece you do not plan to move, you must announce to your opponent that you want to "adjust" a piece's placement. It is also common to use the French word to announce your intention to adjust a piece, by saying "j'adoube" BEFORE touching the piece. You may not adjust a piece unless it is your turn to move. The beginning of the game is always set up as pictured below:

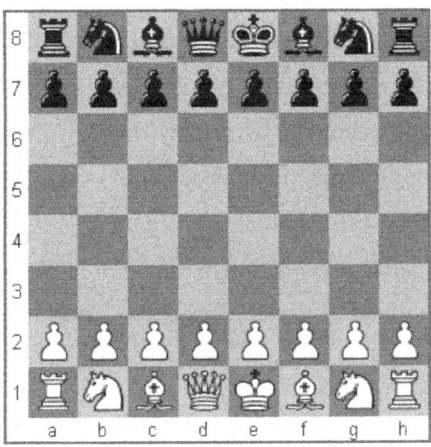

The objective of chess is to checkmate your opponent's King. Do that and you win the game. In the initial set up of the chess board, all pieces should always:

(a) have opposing pieces placed directly opposite from each other in complete symmetry,

(b) be positioned on your chess board with the white square in the lower right corner,

(c) have the white Queen on a white square and the black Queen on a black square.

After your chess board is set up properly, you are now ready to start the game. The key objective is to play all of your chess pieces strategically in order to checkmate the King, while simultaneously protecting your own King from being checkmated. This can be accomplished by making advantageous exchanges, resulting in gaining a "material advantage" over your opponent, which can be converted to a checkmate in the end or by directly attacking and checkmating the opposing King.

The pieces and how they move

To start the game, white always moves first. Each player can then take a turn moving only one piece each turn. You may not move a piece to a square that is already occupied by one of your own pieces. However, you can capture your opponent's piece that stands on a square where one of your pieces can move. In this case, you simply remove your opponent's piece from the board and replace it with your piece. (Note that the only piece which can jump over other pieces is the Knight.)

Memorization

The next important phase of this learning process is for you to memorize what each piece represents and how it moves. Memorizing the pieces and how they move will help you to start understanding and enjoying chess. Don't allow yourself to get overwhelmed or frustrated because you do not understand something right away. Chess takes time to learn. Keep an open mind and be patient. Believe me, I've been there. What matters most is not winning or losing, but playing for fun while you learn. Below you will find basic descriptions of each piece and how they move.

The King

The King is the tallest piece, usually has a cross on top, and is the most important piece in the set. When your King is checkmated, the game is over. Your King can move one square in any direction: up, down, diagonally, and sideways. (See picture below.)

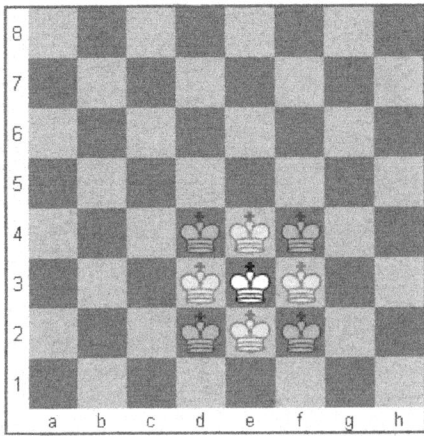

There is one special move the King can make called "castling." You can only castle once in a game. Castling is important because it is a way to put your King into the corner where it can be protected, and it opens the center of the chess board for active play with your other pieces. You castle by moving your King and then Rook. The King should always be touched first when castling.

In castling, you move your King two squares to the left or two squares to the right toward one of your Rooks. Afterward, your Rook goes to the square beside the King. What is critical here is that in order to castle, neither King nor Rook may have been moved before. Also, your King may not castle "out of check," "into check," or "through check." Lastly, for your castle to be considered a legal move neither you nor your opponent may have any other piece between the King and the Rook. Remember, both you and your opponent always have the choice of castling either on the King side or the Queen side of the board, or not at all. (See completed castle move in picture below.)

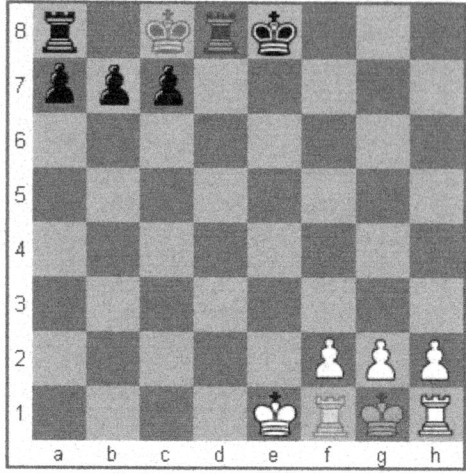

It is illegal to move your King into check; i.e., onto a square being attacked by your opponent's piece. Your King is considered checked when it has been attacked by your opponent and threatened with capture. If you are in check, you must make a move that gets your King out of check immediately. If there is no way to get out of check, you are checkmated and you lose the game.

There are three main ways of getting your King out of check:

(1) Capture your opponent's checking piece.

(2) Place one of your own pieces between your opponent's checking piece and your King, called "interposing" or "blocking the check."

(3) Move your King out of check.

Note that "discovered check" occurs when the opponent moves a piece that unmasks a checking attack from the piece behind it on a row or column or diagonal. "Double check" occurs when there is a discovered check and the unmasking piece is also giving check, resulting in your King being in check in two different ways, i.e., you must move your King when double checked because it is not possible to capture both pieces or interpose a piece that blocks both checking pieces. Double check is a very powerful attacking tactic.

If your King is not in check and you cannot make a legal move with any piece, then your position will be considered a "stalemate," and the game is considered a "draw" or a "tie." "Perpetual check" is also considered a draw and this occurs when your opponent can check you on every move and you cannot avoid the checking sequences. Another way to force a draw is "three-time repetition." This occurs when the same sequence of moves is played three times.

Point Value of Each Piece

The relative value of the chess pieces is also important because it reflects the power of the pieces. The **King** is the **most important piece** and given no numeric value because if you are checkmated you lose the game. You can calculate the value of the pieces you have versus your opponent's pieces to see who is ahead in material. If you are ahead you have a "material advantage."

Material exchanges include the following:

- Being ahead a Pawn or one point is called "a Pawn up."

- Bishops and Knights are both worth 3 points and approximately equal in strength.

- If you capture a Rook worth 5 points with a Bishop or a Knight (each worth 3 points), you are "up and exchange."

- Trading a Rook and a piece (8) for a Queen (9) is not generally recommended unless you get other compensation.

- Trading two Rooks (10) or a Queen (9) can give you a winning advantage if your King is safe from checks by the Queen.

The Queen

The Queen is the second tallest piece in the set, does not have a cross on top, and is the most powerful and dangerous piece in the game. Providing her path is not blocked, your Queen can move any number of squares in any direction: horizontally, vertically, or diagonally. The value of the Queen is 9 points. (See picture below.)

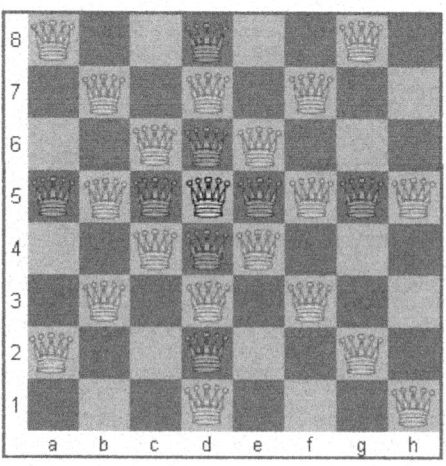

The Rook

The Rook looks like a castle and is called a castle in some parts of the world. It is the next most powerful piece in the game after the Queen. The Rook has a value of 5 points. Providing your Rook's path is not blocked, your Rook can move any number of squares, but only vertically or horizontally, on rows and columns. Rooks are part of the special move, castling, described in the section on the King's movements above. When you castle, not only do you put your King in a safer position, but you also get your Rook more centrally placed. In many situations, connect your Rooks so that they are protecting each other. (See picture below.)

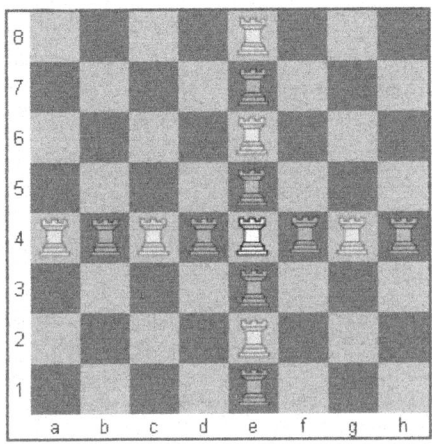

The Knight

The Knight looks like a horse. Its move is considered special because it is the only piece that can jump over the other pieces. Think of the Knight's move as an "L" shape with four squares involved. Specifically, your Knight can be moved directly from its old square to its new square and can jump over other pieces between its old new squares. Your Knight moves two squares horizontally or vertically and then makes a right angle turn for one more square. Your Knight always lands on a square opposite in color from its old square. The Knight is worth 3 points. (See picture below.)

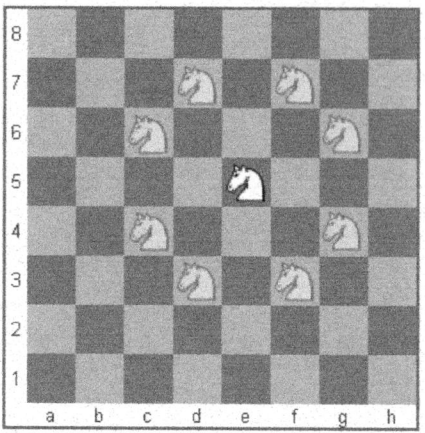

The Bishop

The Bishop has a pointed top and is known as a camel. Providing your Bishop's path is not blocked, you can move your Bishop any number of squares but only diagonally. You start the game with a Bishop on a white square and a Bishop on a black square. Bishops never move to a square of another color, unlike all other pieces in chess. The Bishop is also worth 3 points. (See picture below.)

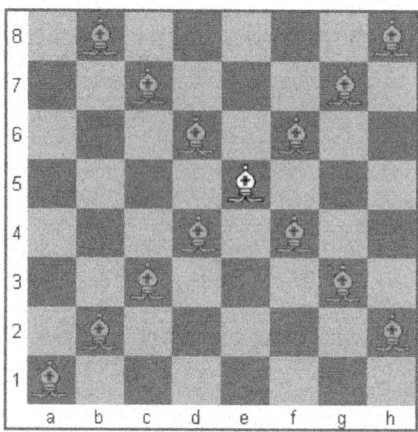

The Pawn

The Pawn is the shortest piece in the set. Your Pawn is the only piece that has a special ability to be promoted and moves just straight ahead and only captures diagonally. For example, your Pawn moves forward one square at a time, but on its very first move in the beginning of the game, it has the option of moving forward one or two squares. The Pawn is worth 1 point. (See picture below)

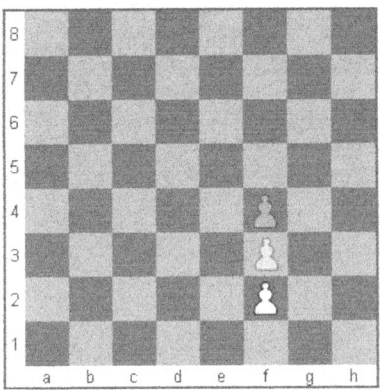

What is unique and special about your Pawn is you can strategically move it to the opposite end of the board, which "promotes" it immediately to another piece—usually the Queen. I love this option because it is possible for you to have more than one Queen or more than two Rooks, Knights, or Bishops on the chess board at the same time. (Note: Your Pawn may not remain a Pawn or become a King.)

With regard to Pawn capture, there is a special move called "**en passant**" which means your Pawn can capture your opponent's Pawn in passing. (En passant is derived from a French phrase which means "in passing" and is used for special Pawn capture only.) En passant occurs when one player moves a Pawn two squares forward to try to avoid capture by the opponent's Pawn. The capture is made exactly as if the player has moved the Pawn only one square forward (See picture for en passant move below). (Note: The white Pawn moved two squares forward to avoid being captured, but the black Pawn has the opportunity to capture the white Pawn via en passant by moving to the black spot.)

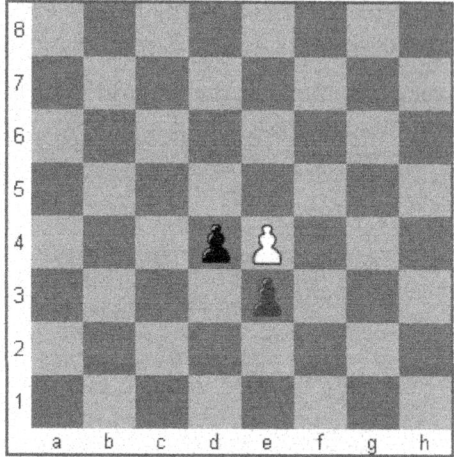

In order for the en passant rule to apply, the following two conditions must be met:

(1) Your opponent's previous move had to be made with a Pawn that advanced two squares from its starting square; or,

(2) The Pawn making an en passant move could have captured an opponent's pawn if it had only advanced just one square versus two squares. Basically, your Pawn is safe from en passant capture for the rest of the game if your opponent does not exercise their right to capture your Pawn initially.

Three main stages of chess

There are three main stages to a chess game: the opening, middle game, and end game. Each stage requires different strategies to play, including taking a stake in the center of the chess board and developing your pieces, King safety, recognizing tactical and strategic ideas for consideration, and converting a material advantage to a win. These relevant stages are outlined below.

Opening: The opening stage is very important and requires your focus so that you don't end up in a cramped and hard to play position. By controlling the center, you gain strength and space over your opponent. Keep in mind the importance of developing your Knights and Bishops early and into the center of the chess board. Your Knights and Bishops do not have to necessarily occupy the four center squares, but they can protect your Pawns while moving forward. It is recommended that you castle in the opening stage to protect your King and complete development of Rooks (either on the King's side or the Queen's side). In castling, you take the King out of its original vulnerable center position and move it to a more protected position. Castling also allows your Rook to be placed in a more central position on the board where it can be more active in your strategic attacks.

Middle Game: In the middle game it is common for exchanges of pieces and Pawns to take place. Be careful not to exchange a piece for another piece worth less, i.e. do not give up a Rook for a Bishop unless you get a mating attack in return or some other compensation for the loss of material. In general, Rooks should occupy open columns. Doubling Rooks on an open column can result in control of the game and limit your opponent's mobility. Also, the middle game is a great time to start identifying, planning, and executing combinations to go directly after your opponent's King. But in order for your combinations to succeed, you need to complete development of your pieces and then place your pieces in their respective strategic positions, which is in harmony with the Pawn structure.

Sometimes, you may find yourself in a position to sacrifice a piece. A **sacrifice** means you intentionally give up a piece of higher value for a much lower value with the expectation of gaining a tactical or strategic advantage over your opponent. While all this is happening, keep a watchful eye on your Pawns. Remember, they still need to be protected since they are potential Queens. Keep in mind that you can lose the game by losing one Pawn and getting nothing in return.

I recommend you read a chess book to learn about common attacking ideas in the middle game and checkmate patterns such as "back rank mate" and "smothered mate." (See Resources for book suggestions in order of difficulty.)

End Game: It is no secret the end game is all about promoting your Pawns to Queens (or sometimes Rooks, Knights, or Bishops—this is an exception, which usually happens in order to avoid a stalemate or a checkmate that can only be prevented by under promotion). As a rule, in the end game, it is good to bring your King out to the center to play a role in the activity. The side with the more active King, minus other factors will win in an end game.

Chess organizations

It is generally important to also familiarize yourself with the two main chess organizations. The first is the United States Chess Federation (USCF), www.uschess.org. The USCF is the official, not-for-profit US membership organization for chess players and chess supporters of all ages and strengths, from beginners to Grandmasters. The USCF represents the United States in the World Chess Federation (FIDE), linking its US members to chess players around the world. If you would like to compete in a chess tournament or find a club in your area, contact the USCF.

The other chess organization is FIDE, the Fédération Internationale des Échecs, which literally translates into the leading World Chess Federation organization. FIDE covers specific regions in the world, including Asia, Europe, Africa, and the Americas. In essence, FIDE is the governing body for world level chess competitions. FIDE also awards players their titles such as Grandmaster or International Master. Their website is www.fide.com.

Final Thoughts

I really hope I have inspired you learn to play chess. Enjoy and be patient with the learning process because the benefits you will gain in the long run are invaluable tools you can use towards success in all your personal and professional endeavors.

> *"Don't be the chess piece—be the SHESS player*
> *and move from Pawn to Queen!"*
>
> —WENDY OLIVERAS, AUTHOR

ABOUT THE AUTHOR

WENDY WAS BORN IN Brooklyn, New York and raised with her siblings in the heart of Manhattan. She is a long-time resident of New Jersey and enjoys playing chess, dancing, hiking, and kayaking when the weather permits.

Since a child, Wendy has had an innate sense of independence and curiosity about learning new things and not being afraid to take chances. Her Daddy taught her how to play chess when she was fourteen years old. She still relies on these invaluable chess instincts and tactical abilities for her own personal and professional successes.

For these reasons, she was inspired to write Checkmate Moves for Business Startups. As an avid chess player, well sought-after small business consultant, published author, motivational public speaker, and leadership trainer, Wendy's passion is fervently fueled by her love for chess and empowering women in business through basic chess strategies for success.

Wendy has evolved into a successful entrepreneur and enjoys teaching and advising others on how to start and grow their businesses. Wendy also enjoys teaching life skills and chess basics to inmates and community-based clients at a corrections and rehabilitation center in New Jersey.

Wendy is the Creative Founder & CEO at SHESS Global Alliance, LLC, and a Small Business Consultant for the New Jersey Small Business Development Center at Rutgers-Newark (RNSBDC). In this role, Wendy provides counseling and mentorship to entrepreneurs and inventors on starting and growing their businesses throughout New Jersey.

She holds an honorary Master's Degree in Human Resources Management, a post-graduate Certification in Career Planning and Development from The New School in New York City, and a Certification in Mental Health First Aid Training. Her background and professional experience encompass the legal recruitment and intellectual property fields, small business consulting, human resources, career mentoring, and educational and leadership training. Her industry focus includes pharmaceuticals, life sciences, biotechnology, engineering, technology, STEM, and litigation.

Wendy believes in giving back to her community. She loves mentoring girls and women to believe in themselves and set and accomplish goals to achieve their life dreams. Wendy believes, together we can all learn new ways to become better planners, thinkers, and decision-makers and accomplish great things.

GREAT RESOURCES

Chess-related Organizations

United States Chess Federation (USCF)
https://new.uschess.org/

World Chess Federation (FIDE)
https://www.fide.com

Have fun and play chess online
https://www.chess.com

New Jersey

New Jersey Business Action Center Hotline – (866) 534-7789

Certification of Minority-Owned and Woman-Owned Business – MBE/
WBE
https://www.sba.gov/starting-business/how-start-business-types/
minority-owned-business

Government Contract Procurement
https://www.sam.gov

Non-Profit Organization – 501 (c)(3)
https://www.state.nj.us/treasury/taxation/rsb100.shtml

The Center for Non-Profits:
http://www.njnonprofits.org/index.html

General Online Business Law
https://www.sba.gov/content/online-business-law

New Jersey Business Incubation Network (NJBIN)
https://www.njbin.org

SHESS Global Alliance, LLC
https://www.shessglobal.com

United States

Federal Licenses and Permits
https://www.sba.gov/content/
what-federal-licenses-and-permits-does-your-business-need

Internal Revenue Service (IRS)
https://www.irs.gov

Library of Congress
https://www.loc.gov

Small Business Administration (SBA)
https://www.sba.gov

Small Business Administration – Women-owned Businesses
https://www.sba.gov/business-guide/grow-your-business/
women-owned-businesses

United States Department of Veterans Affairs
https://www.va.gov/osdbu/

United States Patent and Trademark Office Inventor's Assistance Center (IAC) - (800) 786-9199

United States Patent and Trademark Office (USPTO)
https://www.uspto.gov

United States Small Business Chamber of Commerce
https://www.ussbchamber.org/

United States Women's Chamber of Commerce
https://www.uswcc.org/

Business and Chess-related Books

Anatomy of a Business Plan: The Step-by-Step Guide to Building a Business and Securing Your Company's Future (Small Business Strategies Series), 8th Edition, 2013, by Linda Pinson, Author of the SBA Publication, "How to Write a Business Plan"

"Birth of the Chess Queen: A History" by Marilyn Yalom, 2004

Chess-related Movies

- NETFLIX Series: The Queen's Gambit (2020)

- The Chess Player (2017)

- Queen of Katwe (2016)

- Magnus (2016)

- A Little Game (2014)

- The Dark Horse (2014)

- Pawn Sacrifice (2014)

- Life of a King (2013)

- Brooklyn Castle (2012)

- Bobby Fischer Against the World (2011)

- Queen to Play (2009)

- Knights of the South Bronx (2005)

- Queen of Cactus Cove (2005)

- Game Over: Kasparov and the Machine (2003)

- The Luzhin Defense (2000)

- Chess Kids (1996)

- Long Live the Queen (1995)

- Fresh (1994)

- Searching for Bobby Fischer (1993)

- Knight Moves (1992)